Service Be
By
Brian Campbell Watters

I am indebted to my wife Debra who painstakingly encouraged me in this endeavor and also spent many hours proof reading and making suggestions on content. I also need to express my thanks to my daughter Dr Aurora Watters for her advice on technical aspects of writing and the technical aspect of computer operations. I also owe an enormous debt of gratitude to Nicole Myrie La Chica for her expert guidance and assistance in preparing this book for publication.

Table of Contents

Where It All Began 1
School Life 14
Our History Is In Our Blood 17
Life In A Small Town 23
Pipe Bands 28
The Work Environment 37
Early Working Years 42
The Police Years 46
University Life 74
Foreign Service 79
Posting to British High Commission, Singapore 85
The Love of My Life 92
Royal Visits to Singapore 106
London Posting and Birth of My Darling Daughter Aurora ... 111
Overseas Posting to Tanzania 116
Back to London 142
Overseas Posting to Sri Lanka 143
Cross Posting to Indonesia 151
Life Threatening Illness 165
The Private Sector 170
Indonesia Age of Terrorism 179
Aurora's Higher Education 197
Retirement 201

Aurora Marries Luke Watts.. 209
Round In a Full Circle... 215

The story of a working-class boy born in a small town in the Scottish Borders during World War II and how he made his way through life, improving his education and striving to achieve his dream of service before self by career choices coupled with hard work and dedication. Left school with no educational qualifications, and served an apprenticeship in textile engineering, followed by service in an institute for the blind before joining the police service. With hard work he excelled in his studies in police law and as a result a forward-thinking Chief Constable recognized his potential and sent him off to university to study law where it was suggested he could pass the testing Foreign Office recruitment process. His application to join the foreign service was successful and his first overseas posting was to Singapore where he was a guest of honor at a charity fashion show and was captivated by a former Miss Singapore who was one of the models and spent six months looking for her before they eventually met up on a blind date. In just over a year, they were married and went off round the world on a three-month honeymoon. He served further Foreign Office postings in Tanzania, Sri Lanka, and Indonesia. After retirement he set up a private company dedicated to protecting companies from the dangers of international terrorism in Indonesia and explaining the acute difference between contingency plans suitable for company operations in the west and those suitable for operations in the third world.

Where It All Began

The dark clouds of war were the backdrop for my birth in the small town of Hawick in the Scottish Borders. Indeed, the war and its aftermath, together with the small-town ethos, were to be a constant feature of my early years and probably played a major part in developing my character and attitude to life. We were not rich in the materialistic sense, but I was endowed with a loving and caring environment both in terms of life within my own family and life in the greater family of that unique small border town where everybody knew everybody else and where there was an unbelievable rich tapestry of caring and friendship.

The war of course meant absences by my father who was serving overseas in the Royal Air Force, flying Sunderland flying boats out of Iceland escorting the transatlantic convoys shipping war supplies from the US to the UK.

My Parents' Wedding

My grandparents were always there in the background and, indeed, in many ways in the foreground, and one of my earliest memories was of spending many happy days staying in their small house in the centre of the town where I happily slept on the floor on a throw-down mattress. My grandfather had fought in the first world war but was too old to serve in the second world war and was, therefore, there as an anchor for my formative years. I cannot remember much of the actual war – I do have a vague memory of a gas mask, or rather a sort of gas incubator that I would be placed in should gas attacks occur – but otherwise was blissfully unaware of the great suffering and deprivation that befell our population. The fact that the main industry of our little town was cashmere and lambswool high-quality knitwear and was not directly involved in the war effort ruled it out as a priority target for German bombers, although I do remember after the war, some unexploded ordinance was found in the hills surrounding the town.

At the time of my birth, we lived in a small attic in the middle of the town, and although it was simple, it was a home and a loving one. However, after the end of the war, the government built a development of prefabricated houses on the edge of the town. They were simple in construction and made of asbestos, but they did boast such luxuries as a fireplace with a back burner boiler that heated the water, a gas fridge and a bathroom complete with a bathtub. This might not seem like much of a luxury in this day and age, but the fact was that even after the war, many homes in the town did not have a bathroom, and indeed many had outside toilets. My grandparents lived in such a house and I remember freezing in the middle of winter when using the outside toilet. Indeed, it was the practice in winter to leave an oil lamp burning in the toilet during winter nights to prevent the water pipes from freezing. Without a bath or shower, many inhabitants were reduced to having a daily strip wash at the kitchen sink and once a week heading off to the town swimming baths where one could rent a hot bath for an hour and luxuriate in piping hot water. The public baths also provided a communal wash house where one could take the weekly washing and not only have it washed but also dried in huge driers.

My grandmother had a wash house at the end of the garden, which housed a huge copper vessel which was heated by firewood and was used to boil the whites. Colors were washed at a cooler temperature in the sink in the wash house and were scrubbed on a wooden scrubbing board to loosen the dirt. Monday was prescribed as the wash day, and rain or shine that was the day when she would carry out the weekly wash. If there was no sun to dry the clothes on the washing line, they would be brought indoors to be dried over a couple of days by the open coal fire. Those who did not enjoy the luxury of their own wash house made their weekly trek to the town wash house with their washing bundled up in an old pram. Old prams had another use as they were used by some to visit the gas works where coke, a byproduct of gas extraction, could be purchased and hauled home in the pram. This fuel was cheaper than coal and was a popular means of heating homes. It should be noted that most families did not have a car and old prams were a common method of moving goods on what were essential journeys.

However, I digress. Moving back to our prefabricated houses or prefabs as they were commonly known, it must be said that they lacked a suitable level of insulation. It was common in the winter to get up in the morning to find ice on the INSIDE of the windows. In spite of these drawbacks, the prefabs were self-contained, and we all had a front and back garden and an Anderson air raid shelter in the back garden, which with the outbreak of peace, became the coal cellar and general storeroom for garden implements, etc. Our prefab only had two bedrooms, so my parents slept in the bigger one and my sister in the smaller one, and I had to bed down on a sofa in the living room.

In spite of the houses being detached and self-contained, there was a wonderful spirit of community, and most of the inhabitants didn't even bother to lock the doors to their homes. After the travails of war, our community was content to live a simple but happy life, and the back gardens were soon planted out with fruit and vegetables, including our staple food, the humble potato. Many gardens were planted with new potatoes or earlies, which ripened in the spring and were generally eaten cold as part of a salad – the lettuce and spring onions in the salad also came fresh from the garden. The front gardens largely consisted of a lawn with borders laid out with hardy flowering plants. Owing to our financial situation, we didn't buy fertilizer for the garden, but I was sent off at a very early age with a bucket to collect sheep droppings from the surrounding farmland, which were mixed with water and used as a natural and, more importantly, free fertilizer.

Typical Prefab

The prefabs were situated on the northern extremity of the town. They gave easy access to thousands of acres of fields and rolling hills, which soon became our "playground" where we spent many happy hours playing self-made games which often consisted of one team setting off into the hills and hiding in the gorse bushes with the other team setting off to find them. This was more than a childish game of hide and seek as, in effect, it provided us with lots of healthy exercise and the opportunity to explore the wealth of natural beauty in the countryside and the ways of the wild. There was always the harvest of the hedgerows at our disposal, and wild crab apples, wild gooseberries, wild raspberries and nuts were there just for the plucking. With wartime food rationing, which carried on for many years after the war, our diet was simple and basic, but in fact, many nutritionists now say that the simple low-cholesterol diet was without doubt much healthier than the modern diet of fast food and prepackaged meals. That diet, coupled with plenty of fresh air and exercise, was regarded as the norm and suited us just fine, and we never felt that we were deprived to any degree.

Indeed, the harvest of the hedgerows went even further than providing us with snacks, and in the summer, family excursions were organized where the whole family went picking wild raspberries, gooseberries and crab apples, which were later made into homemade jam to see us through the winter months. I remember one such expedition where we picked wild raspberries with a Government National Dried Milk tin hanging round our necks into which we placed the precious fruit.

Government National Dried Milk tin

It wasn't without its dangers, especially when you were small, as the wild nettles towered over our heads, ready to sting with the slightest touch. These homemade preserved foods were important to us, and there was much saving of food rationing coupons to ensure that we could purchase sufficient sugar for jam making. (Indeed, in my youth, we were not allowed to purchase sweets as almost the entire sugar ration allowance was reserved for sugar for jam making.) The scarcity of sugar was probably responsible for my habit of drinking tea without sugar and milk, even to this day. Rationing affected our lives in many ways, and I recall after the war queuing outside the local Cooperative Store for three hours for four oranges, which was my first taste of that fruit at the age of about six years!

Television was in its infancy, and we certainly could not afford one, but we didn't really miss the small screen sets with poor reception and a picture obscured by snow-like interference. We did have a radio which was much used in winter evenings when we sat round the fire as a family listening to really good quality programmes. But on the whole, we youths were outdoor creatures roaming the hills around the town, and during the long school summer holidays, were rarely to be found at home, as we spent much of our waking and sleeping hours camping out in tents in a nearby field.

Total freedom coupled with simple pleasures and a vivid youthful imagination allowed us to act out what we imagined the life of soldiers in war to have been. As we matured, the romance of war time receded as we learned from ex-servicemen the horrors of war. However, in many ways, the war was still around us in early peacetime as former soldiers would spell out just how damnable wars really were and stripped away the glory from our youthful eyes. Ex-service clubs were popular and, in many ways, allowed former combatants to avoid combat stress disorders through fellowship but that was only the formal side and a group of former military men, some with Chindit and special forces experience, took an interest in us youths. They set aside time from their own lives to spend time with us youngsters, guiding us through these youthful years. At the time, we didn't see it as such and were more interested in the lessons they gave us on how to live off the land and how to bring a military element of orderliness to our shamble of a campsite. Tents were no longer erected in a disorderly way but set out in orderly lines. Campfires were properly set with a ring of stones to avoid the spread of fire, rubbish was collected and buried, and tents moved location every few days to allow the grass to recover.

We were taught to live in harmony with nature and to appreciate how it could best serve our interests. Although it was great fun, they were, in effect, introducing us to the discipline that they had acquired through army life with the result that it became the norm in our daily lives. Good timekeeping, honesty and care for our fellows became a foundation for us during our formative years and beyond. I salute these far-thinking men for giving their time and effort to set us on the right path. I suppose, in many ways, this was a benefit derived from the small-town life where we were part of a community from which we obtained great benefit whilst, at the same time, following the example of others, we learned to give back to that same community.

There was little traffic in our housing estate, and another pastime was to play football in the street with jumpers placed on the ground to mark the goal area.

This was just after the war, and a short distance away from our prefabricated houses, there was a POW camp for

German Prisoners of war. Amazingly, we young kids were allowed to wander in and out of the camp, which was quite open, and chat to the prisoners.

German POW camp

We got great satisfaction from making our own entertainment, and in the winter months, we got great pleasure from sledging when snow was on the ground. We lived in a hilly area with plenty of slopes to sledge on. Some were gentle, but others were, with hindsight, quite dangerous, especially as we would rope several sledges together to form a snake of sledges that we called a "yokatola." We would play in the snow until our hands were blue from the cold, but that was a price we were happy to pay for these simple pleasures. Our sledges were homemade, and we went to the local blacksmith to have the metal runners made, and we screwed them onto our home-made wooden sledges. I suppose we lived in an era where we used our ingenuity to provide for our needs, a far cry from today's consumerism. We also constructed homemade go-karts which we called bogies, and the same slopes that provided propulsion through gravity for our winter sledging became our go-kart racetracks. In these modern times, the Health and Safety Brigade would outlaw such activities, and although accidents did happen, we didn't allow them to curb our enthusiasm. Indeed, life was simpler then, and we were less hidebound by regulation.

There was a stream, a runoff from the hills, running through the area that we played in called Bonny Burn (Pretty Stream) with crystal clear water. In the summer, we spent many happy hours playing in that stream even though the water was quite cold. The stream wasn't really deep, but we managed to dam one area making it deep enough to swim. Upstream from the area where we played was a lean-to made up of old and rusty corrugated steel sheets and foliage that was home to a tramp who was known as Tammy Swunt (Tommy Swinton). He was a casualty of the war and never managed to re-join society when he returned home. He lived summer and winter in this lean-to, and we were all quite scared of him. He obviously had a mental problem and would shout and curse at us youngsters, probably the result of drinking cheap wine! He was one of the casualties of WW2 and, in modern terms, could be said to be suffering from traumatic stress disorder. Still, in those days, the term was unheard of, and social services were not really capable of dealing with such situations. So, he lived, summer and winter, in this hovel, seemingly unaffected by extreme cold, but I suspect that he did suffer from the climatic conditions. Looking back, he was more sinned against than being a sinner.

Growing Up

We were all quite good swimmers as we went to the local public baths after school two days a week at a special school rate. The baths master taught us how to swim, and in addition to luxuriating in the hot tub, we did manage to swim lengths of the pool. The route from the school to the public baths took us down what was referred to as the hundred steps, a long narrow stone staircase consisting of just short of 100 steps. It was great to run down but we also had a system whereby we would try to run up all the way to the top on the way home leaving us in a heap of sweat and panting when we got to the top. Swimming was important as the town had two major rivers running through it. When we were a little older, we regularly swam in these major rivers, which were crystal clear, and we enjoyed hours of fun from this simple activity.

The Hundred Steps

In those days, the High Street of the town was not covered in tarmac, and the surface was made up of granite squares which had been laid down many years earlier. This surface suited the horse traffic, and the local cooperative store used horse and carts for both milk and groceries deliveries. There was also a Scottish transport and delivery company, Mutter-

Howie, that exclusively used horse-drawn vehicles for general deliveries, many of which were connected with the town's woolen industry. The milk delivery horses were quite smart and knew just where to stop as the milkman went off with full bottles and returned with empties. The horses would then walk on to the next point, at which the milkman would again set off with deliveries, and so it went on.

Although it was, in effect, the end of the horse-drawn era, many farmers in the area still used horses in addition to tractors. The draught horses were usually Clydesdales which were powerful, standing up to 18 hands in height and weighing up to 2000 pounds. With their measured gait and feathered legs, they were a sight to behold, and these gentle giants were well suited in strength and temperament for town and country use. I was lucky enough to have a friend whose father had a farm, and I loved to spend weekends on the farm with him and his family. Their day began very early, and at first light (in the winter, even before first light), we were up and about letting out and feeding hens and then mucking out and feeding their two Clydesdale horses called Bob and Jean. After this, cows were milked and then and only then, we repaired to the farmhouse for a hot breakfast in the enormous kitchen. Home-cured hams hung from the ceiling, and generous slices were soon fried up with either duck or hens' eggs accompanied by home-baked bread and hot tea. During the summer months, life on the farm was great for us youngsters, and although we were expected to do our fair share of the work, especially at harvest time, we did have a lot of fun working the horses and being taught how to drive their small tractor. The small tractor was a sign of things to come and a signal that the end of the horse-drawn era was in sight.

The winters were quite harsh, and we had more than our fair share of snow. When walking to school (not for us the luxury of parents chauffeuring us to and from school), we found ourselves trudging through snow that could be quite deep. However, we found a benefit in these conditions and slopes on the route were soon converted into icy slides, which provided some merriment on the walk to and from school. Our primary school was about a mile and a half away (our secondary school was well over two miles away), but it never seemed to be a chore as we never walked alone and enjoyed the company of our peers, forging friendships that have lasted until today.

School Life

In school life, we also encountered discipline. Rather than the self-discipline taught by the former soldiers, we had discipline imposed from above, and woe betide anyone who broke the rules. Teachers were demigods whose word was law, and although it seemed quite draconian at the time, with hindsight, it was a good grounding for life. Discipline was enforced by the use of a thick leather belt that was administered to our hands. This type of corporal punishment was tough but effective and looking back on it, I don't believe it did us any harm.

Not for us the hallowed towers of public school but a simple and effective education with strong emphasis on the three Rs. Today, when I write long papers with pie charts that I send electronically around the world, it is with some amusement that my mind goes back to life in my first primary school class, where we were issued a slate, an Oxo tin filled with chalk and a duster, which were our tools for the task of learning to write. Interestingly enough, our Primary One teacher rejoiced in the name "Miss Virtue" – how apt.

Wilton Primary School

School photo circa 1950 – I am far right back row

Our teachers were strict but fair, and the better ones did manage to capture our imagination and inspire a thirst for learning. I certainly owe that dedicated band of teachers a huge debt of gratitude and happily was able to express it in person when two former teachers from Hawick High School turned up at our fiftieth anniversary of graduating from high school. I say graduating, but in effect, there was no graduation as such, and we just left school and went on to a job. (In those days, graduation was confined to universities and it does seem strange when nowadays even kids graduate from primary schools complete with academic gowns.) Whilst it was an experience to meet with my peers and learn what they had achieved in their lives, the greater pleasure came from meeting these teachers almost on an equal footing and having the opportunity to thank them for their untiring efforts. It is worthy of note that they took a great interest in learning what we had done with our lives and of our achievements. I suppose I was what is often referred to as a late developer. I must admit that I regret not having taken full advantage of tuition in my primary years, but when I reached high school, I realised that it was up to me to ensure that I achieved a good education and not rely on being cajoled by teachers.

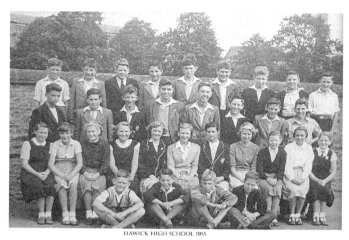

I am second from right back row

Hawick High School

Our History Is In Our Blood

One of the advantages of small-town living was the sense of fellowship and shared history, and this was certainly the case in my hometown. The Scottish borders suffered many centuries of strife as the border between England and Scotland moved north and south over the years. It is often said that hardship can result in a more determined and resolute people, and I like to think that this was the case not only in my hometown of Hawick, but was an important element in towns throughout the Borders as the townsfolk looked after each other.

This resoluteness in the Border towns was founded in history. In 1513, the English Army defeated the Scots at the battle of Flodden Moor and in early 1514, part of the English army, seeking spoils of war, came through my hometown, and many other Border towns and ransacked them. They were able to do so largely unimpeded in my hometown as most of the men in the town had been killed on Flodden Field, and the young men of the town, who were too young to join the battle, were out in the fields some distance from the town attending to farming duties, which they had taken over from their fathers who had lost their lives in the battle. In the evening, when they came home to the town and witnessed the dreadful devastation of pillage by the English Army, they delved deep into their souls and mounted their workhorses and rode after that part of the English army which had camped about three miles outside the town under a bridge by the river Teviot known as Horneshole Bridge.

The English soldiers probably saw no threat and had not posted sentries, and as a result, they fell to these young men who routed them and captured their flag, which was the blue and gold banner of the Abbot of Hexam. They rode back to the town carrying the flag and were rightly received as heroes. A local landowner, the Earl of Drumlanrig, was so incensed by the heroic act of these young men that he gave land to the town, which was to be regarded as common land upon which the townsfolk were free to cut peat and graze their livestock. The grant of land was in perpetuity but there was a condition which was that the young unmarried men of the town were required to ride the boundaries of the land once a year. The riding of the boundaries of the common land gave way to a tradition in the form of a festival which was to become known as the Common Riding i.e., the riding of the common land boundaries, and I am pleased and proud to say that this tradition has continued until today. In 1914 on the 400th anniversary of the battle of Horneshole Bridge, a local sculptor created a bronze statue of the leader of this group of boys riding his horse triumphantly back into the town bearing the banner. The statue was erected in the centre of the town, and in 2014 the statue was refurbished and unveiled again on the 1st of May at 14 minutes past eight in the evening. Thus, the second unveiling was carried out on 1.5.14 at 2014 in the evening, thus cleverly marking the occasion using the first and current dates of the 500 years of the tradition. Sadly, William Beattie, the sculptor who crafted the statue, was killed in battle in the First World War.

The tradition has it that each year a young unmarried man of the town is chosen to lead the Common Riding in a position known as the Cornet, effectively representing the young unmarried youths who had routed the English Army. In this role, he is supported by an older married man who is known as the Acting Father, keeping alive the tradition after the Battle of Flodden, whereby the elders of the town who were too old to join the Scottish Army acted as a father or guardian to the orphaned youth of the town. Interestingly, many other local traditions have been grafted onto the Common Riding festival, including the wearing of an oak leaf on one's jacket, perhaps as a continuation of an old Druid practice. The festival lasts for six weeks, and the final week takes place in the first full week of June when a girl chosen by the Cornet as his lass busses the flag, also known as the Colour, by tying a blue and gold ribbon onto the flag after which it is presented to the Cornet by the town Provost who charges the young man to faithfully ride the boundaries of the common land and return the flag unsullied and unstained. Even during times of war and, more recently pandemic, the boundaries have been ridden by local officials.

Hawick is a small town of fewer than 16,000 souls, but each year more than 400 of its youth mount their horses and follow the Cornet when he carries out his duties. I am proud to say that I was one of those young men, and when I first took part, I was inducted into the Ancient Order of Mosstroopers and entitled to wear its badge of membership. (The Mosstroopers were essentially those Hawick men who rode around the area recovering cattle stolen by the English, although I should add that they also stole English cattle!) Folklore has it that the wife of the head of a Border family would tell her husband that the larder was empty by serving him with a dinner plate that was devoid of food but instead contained a pair of spurs meaning that it was time to ride the moss and steal some cattle to replenish the larder! The tie worn by Mosstroopers is green with red and gold and is said to represent the green of the moss that they trooped, the red for the blood that was spilt and the gold for the golden sunrise when they returned to the town. In my youth, the followers of the Cornet were entirely male, thus representing the young men who took on the English Army. However, in these days of political correctness, women are also allowed to take part, and I am convinced that the inclusion of women riders has not only swelled the numbers but has also made the festivities a more truly community occasion.

However, long before I was able to afford to ride behind the cornet, I was able to take part to a degree by being one of the many poor Hawick young men who earned a small amount of money by riding on our bicycles to the location of the ride out on each Saturday to act as a sort of groom, by looking after the riders' mounts whilst they were involved in non-mounted activities (drinking beer). This suited us fine as we were paid a small sum for our trouble. In fact, there was also another hidden benefit to acting as guardian of horses and I benefitted from this fact. I eventually got myself a job as the guardian of a horse owned by a local stonemason whose business demands meant that he was unable to ride in all the ceremonies and when he was tied up with business, he kindly allowed me to ride his horse on those days free of charge. This suited me fine and in return I would spend some of my free time visiting the stables where he kept his horse and carry out grooming and general stable cleaning duties. In time I was able to afford to hire a horse for my own use for the 6 weeks of the festivities and fully participated in all events.

Me looking after the pony of Drew Martin, who went on to lead the ceremonies as Cornet

Common Riding Saturday 1961. I am second from the left.

The deeds of these young Hawick men in 1514 are not only marked by the Common Riding Festival but also in song and verse. From an early age, we children learned these songs, and many of us could sing the words by heart, of up to 30 of these songs, depicting not only the bravery of those young men, but also the attributes of the town that we all loved. The following verse, paraphrased from one of these songs, perfectly encapsulates the spirit of the town and the Common Riding. "It's not in steeds, it's not in speeds, but something in the heart abiding. It's kindly customs, words and deeds, it's these that make the Common Riding."

Life In A Small Town

There are no doubt pluses and minuses in living in a small town of less than 16,000 inhabitants, but overall, I believe the pluses exceed the minuses by far. One didn't have to look far when in need of assistance, as most folk in the town knew or knew of the majority of the population.

The main street, the High Street, is less than a mile long, but on a Saturday morning, it could take a very long time to get from one end to the other. As you came across people, you knew it was not enough to simply wave and walk past, but you were essentially obliged to spend some time chatting with them, be it about the weather, the rugby, or merely local gossip.

High Street with Town Hall in the background

I should add that these chats were not in the English language but in a local patois or dialect peculiar to the town. An example of this is that there are two words for the word you, ee and yow. For example, if I were going to say, "you can go," I would say, "ee can gan," and if I wanted to say, "I will give it to you," I would say, "A'll geed tae yow." Suffice it to say that we were brought up using the patois, but once we went to school, we had to master the English language.

You would stop to chat with one person, then a friend of his would join you, and then a friend of the friend, and so on. The world had to be put right, and you were certainly the people who knew just what would be required to make it so. An accident or illness affecting someone you didn't know would result in a lengthy dissertation that explained that his family were related to so and so's family, and that family was one that you might have heard of. During these discussions, the maiden names of women had to be gone through to identify them or their children, and this who's who was trotted out every Saturday morning. By lunchtime you were ready for a beer, and after a couple of pints and a couple of mutton pies, it was time to stroll down the side of the river Teviot to watch the Hawick Rugby club playing, if they had a home match. If they had an away match, the townsfolk would make the journey to support their team by bus or, for the wealthier, by car.

Rugby in those days was a very different game from what we witness today. It was purely an amateur sport, and the game was played for the love of the game. The question of what you could put into the game was far more important than what you could get out of the game. In fact, in those days, the second point would never come to mind. Border rugby was the setting for inter-town rivalry, and this was especially so when the seven-a-side tournaments were held at the end of each summer prior to the 15 a side fixtures, and again at the end of the season when the spring sevens were held.

The seven-a-side game was invented by Ned Haig in the nearby border town of Melrose and whilst there are no written records, tradition relates that in 1883 the Melrose Rugby Football Club was looking for ideas to raise funds for the club and hit upon a knock out tournament involving only seven players on each side. The first such tournament was held in Melrose that year, and before long other border towns initiated their own seven tournaments. There is also a rival claim that Ned Haig invented the game as means of getting his players fit for the season after a long summer of overindulgence.

The famous rugby commentator Bill McLaren was a native of Hawick, and following what was common for us all in our youth, he played rugby. Bill saw service in uniform with the Royal Artillery during WW2 in Italy and, after the war, resumed playing rugby. He played for the famous Hawick Rugby Club. He played alongside my uncle Jim Dalgetty and was good enough that he played in a trial for the Scottish national team in 1947 and was on the verge of playing for the national team. The same year whilst playing for Hawick, my uncle pointed out to him that he was slow and was behind the play for most of the game. Bill said that he was having trouble breathing and, indeed, left the field of play during the game. On the Monday morning, he went to see the doctor, and he was admitted to a sanatorium in East Fortune in Scotland, where he spent 19 months suffering from TB. My uncle related that Bill was not expected to survive the dreadful disease but was approached by the doctors and asked if he would be willing to serve as a guinea pig in a trial of a new and not yet fully tested drug, streptomycin. He readily agreed and was one of only two volunteers who survived. During his recovery, he began his commentary career by broadcasting on table tennis games on the hospital radio. He began his rugby commentating career with BBC Radio Scotland, and in my youth, when we visited the house of a friend who owned a TV, we would switch off the TV sound and listen to Bill's commentary on the radio. After six years with BBC Radio, he switched to TV and became the most famous rugby commentator of all time and was awarded an MBE in 1992, an OBE three years later, and a CBE in 2003. Many of us are of the opinion that his success as a TV commentator was that during his radio days, he developed a skill in making the game come alive for listeners who were unable to see the actual play. In addition to his commentating, he became a PE teacher and taught in many Scottish schools until the age of 64. He taught many Hawick youngsters who went on to play for Scotland.

Bill is one of a long line of sons of Hawick who became famous. Another was James Wilson, who founded the Economist Magazine and the now defunct Chartered Bank of India in the 19th century.

More recently, another son of Hawick, Sir Chay Blyth CBE, BEM, rose to fame. He joined the British Army Parachute Regiment at 18 and was promoted to Sergeant by the age of 21. He came to prominence in 1966 when, together with Capt. John Ridgway, he rowed across the North Atlantic in a 20-foot open boat in 92 days. From a complete novice, he went on to forge a career in sailing, and in 1971 he became the first person to sail nonstop westwards around the world aboard the yacht British Steel.

Back to my family now. My Great Grandmother played the piano to accompany the silent movies in local cinemas, and my grandfather and his brother were both musicians. I was expected to follow the tradition and was sent off for piano lessons. Sad to say, the piano was not for me as I simply was not cut out for it. I did, however, have a good singing voice and, over the years, progressed from boy soprano through tenor, baritone, and then bass. In my boy soprano days, I sang in the church choir and was good enough to take the lead in the many operettas that were put on in the church hall for the pleasure of the congregation. Amazingly to this day, I still remember the lyrics perfectly, which I suppose is testament to hours of preparation and practice. Furthermore, in my teenage years, I joined the Hawick Amateur Operatic Society and took part in many musical productions.

Pipe Bands

My teen years were packed with wonderful opportunities free from the distractions of laptops, iPads, and the internet. I joined the Life Boys and graduated from there to the Boys Brigade when I reached the age of 12 years. Looking back these organisations were able to provide me with a stable platform on which to build my life. They provided another genus of discipline where teamwork and service before self came into my life. Once again, I applaud the efforts of those volunteers who willingly gave up their own time to set us youngsters on the right path. I should especially mention the captain of the 4th Hawick Company of the Boys Brigade, Drew Linton, who gave of his time most willingly to provide an educational and moral backdrop for us young men.

A group taken at the 21st birthday party of the 4th Hawick Company of the Boys' Brigade. 1955

I am 4th from the left middle row and Drew Linton is in the middle of the front row

I also joined the Hawick Boys Brigade Pipe Band and graduated from being a drummer to becoming the Drum Major of the band. This was a real life-changing experience, and thanks to the herculean efforts of Pipe Major Bob Short, we wild young men were transformed into a disciplined group able to perform for all levels of society.

We practiced two nights a week with another night devoted to the 4th Hawick Company of the Boys Brigade, which meant that three nights in the week were filled with character-building activities. In the winter months, we practiced in a large public hall in the town, but as soon as the clocks changed in the spring, we practiced outdoors on Duke Street that ran between the hall and the River Teviot. Many townspeople came out to watch and listen, and, I suppose in a small way, we provided some free entertainment for them.

The Band on an Overseas assignment – I am 2nd from the right

In addition to these practice nights, we went out on engagements, some big and some small. We regularly played at country shows around both the north and south of the Scottish border with England and played a full part in the community life of our hometown of Hawick. Armistice Sunday was a hectic day when I left home early in the morning to play the Last Post and Reveille on the bugle at Armistice services at two small towns some 30 miles from Hawick. As a matter of interest, one of these services was close to the grave of the great F1 World Champion Jim Clark at Chirnside. Then it was back to Hawick, where I led the band for the town's armistice service in the beautiful surroundings of the town's park at the WW1 and WW2 memorial and afterwards at the Boer War memorial. I also played the Last Post and Reveille for the Gallipoli Comrades once a year on their anniversary and watched the number of comrades drop off year upon year (an experience that was echoed in 2014 at the 70th anniversary of the D-Day landings when the numbers of veterans still alive were few and reducing).

I entered the Scottish Borders Boys Brigade Bugle championship and was declared Champion. I was up against, among others, a trumpet player from a brass band, and his bugle sounded sweet, but the judge, who was ex-military, said that bugle calls were in effect commands and my rendering was more commanding! Dislocation of expectation.

Mrs Joan Symonds, B.B.C. Producer, briefs the boys for a television appearance from the Manchester studios.
[Photo: Hawick News]

I am 4th from right

However, our pipe band engagements weren't all small-town work, and we toured in Europe, where we played on the same bill as the then popular singer Helen Shapiro and the well-known American group, The Platters.

The World Famous Singing Group, the Platters from the U.S.A., pictured with some of the boys during a rehearsal for a Radio Programme from Stockholm.

I am third from the left next to Herb Reed, the base singer who created the name Platters, as that was what DJs called vinyl records.

Herb was great fun and was so down to earth. On one occasion, we were chatting after a gig when a group of girls rushed towards us with autograph books. Herb said that it would only take him a minute, but he laughed when the girls ran past him and came to me resplendent in my kilt.

These tours took us to Denmark, Sweden, Holland and France and in each location, we were well received as the skirl of the pipes, and the sight of a kilted pipe band were regarded as something of a spectacle. Some of the enthusiasm was no doubt engendered by the fact that Scottish Regiments played a part in the liberation of some of these countries during the 2nd world war. These tours during my teenage years provided me with the privilege and honor of representing my town by leading the band in these exciting locations and was once again a character-building experience.

Me leading the Hawick Boys Brigade Pipe Band in Holland

Photo of the entire Band. I am on the left of the anchor.

Malmo Airport, Sweden. I am extreme right.

Hawick 1956. I am 3rd from right, middle row.

I am extreme right

The Lord Mayor of Groningen, Holland, talks to the Tenor Drummers during a Reception in the City Chambers, 1959.

I am 3rd from the left

The Con Amore Choir from Copenhagen and the Band, photographed admiring the Floral Crest of The Boys' Brigade in Newcastle. [Photo: Newcastle Journal]

I am 2nd from the right

The Work Environment

Going back a little, I left school at the age of 15. I went to work as an apprentice engineer at the world-famous knitwear company Lyle and Scott and the two pounds one shilling and sixpence a week I initially earned was a welcome addition to my family's income. My Grandfather worked for this company for fifty-five years except for the time he spent fighting in France during the First World War.

My Grandfather training a young apprentice

The woolen industry provided a fair living wage for its workforce, and in return, many of the workers served the company from leaving school until retirement. Indeed, my grandfather worked until he was seventy when he retired, and I carried on the family history in the company. My Grandfather, Jack Campbell, known as Jek, was a gentleman in the truest sense of the word and I never heard him speak ill of anyone. As mentioned earlier, his mother had been a pianist in the silent movie halls and he and his brother Alec, known as Eck, inherited her love of music. They had a small orchestra where he played the piano and his brother the violin, and in their spare time, they played at dances and other events. Although his name was Jack, he was known as Jeck, so the two band leaders were referred to as Jeck and Eck.

My Grandfather and Grandmother in the back row and his brother Alec and his wife in front

As was common in those less affluent days, I also had a part-time job serving in a local bar on my free evenings, thereby supplementing my meagre income. I also had a Sunday morning newspaper round to bring in extra cash. One of the bars I worked in had a landlord who was fond of drink, and his wife, who ran the bar with him, tried with a limited degree of success to control the amount of alcohol he consumed. Scottish bars in those days were very much a male preserve, but most had a small separate bar where women could drink in semi-private with their husbands or girlfriends cosseted from the rather uncouth atmosphere of the main bar. The small bar, often known as the snug bar, didn't have a full-time bartender but was equipped with a bell that one could use to ring for service. On one occasion, I spotted the landlord go into the snug bar, greet the occupants and enquire what drinks they wanted. He then went off into the main bar and returned with the drinks on a tray. He later returned to the main bar with the empty glasses and bottles, and only I knew that there were in fact, no customers and that he had consumed the drinks himself in the closeted area. On another occasion, the cistern in the bar toilet broke down, and I had to accompany the plumber who was called in to repair it. Imagine our surprise when we found two unopened bottles of extra strong beer nestled in the cistern, ready for him to consume when the coast was clear!

The bars and private clubs in the town provided great fellowship, and many ex-servicemen found this fellowship a great way to get over the horrors of the war. After the war, my father was a member of the Royal Air Force Association, which had a branch in the town, and the British Legion and Ex-servicemen's clubs were popular venues for those who had served in the war. When I was 17, and therefore still under the legal drinking age, my grandfather took me along with him to the Annual Club Dinner at the local Ex-servicemen's club. I had always hidden the fact that I was already drinking alcohol at that time, but my father and grandfather both knew that I liked a drink. Anyway, we arrived at the Club and my grandfather bought me a whisky which I was very much enjoying when the bell went for us to sit down to dinner. I found that the placement had me sitting next to a Church of Scotland Minister, and my heart sank (Church of Scotland Ministers had a reputation for being anti-drink, like their Baptist colleagues). The Minister looked at my drink and in what seemed like a stern voice, he asked, "Is that whisky you're drinking, young man?" I rather hesitantly replied that it was indeed whisky whereupon he said, "Do you think it would be cheaper if we bought a half bottle of whisky between us rather than buying singles all evening?" A perfect example of dislocation of expectation!

Early Working Years

As mentioned earlier, I served as an apprentice textile engineer with the famous knitwear company Lyle and Scott. I had always wanted to join the Police service, but my father insisted (as many fathers in that era did) that I "get a trade". I found my years as an apprentice engineer in the factory an enriching experience, and I am pleased to see that apprenticeships are coming back into vogue. In return for learning a trade, I was at the beck and call of the experienced journeymen, and as I was the younger of two apprentices, I was the lowest form of life! The chief engineer was a wonderful man called Adam Balmer, who was strict but at the same time treated me as he would a son. On a Friday at 5 p.m., he would gather all the engineers around him with mugs of tea for a review of the past week and to plan the following week. As I was the youngest apprentice, I was not allowed to join this august group but had to go around the engineering shop cleaning down all the machinery. When I declared that all the machines were clean, Adam would come around and inspect each machine, and if he spotted any defects, I would be soundly admonished.

On one occasion when all the machines were declared suitably clean, he asked me what I was going to do for the weekend. I told him that I was coming in to work on Saturday as one of the machines needed some maintenance. He told me to go and bring him a bucket of water, and when I put it down in front of him, he told me to put my hands into the water. I looked at him with incredulity, and he snapped that I should do as he said and put my hands in the water, which I duly did. He then asked me to take my hands out of the water, and when I did so, he said that the hole left behind when I took my hands out was as much as I would be missed if I didn't come into work over the weekend. His point was that no one was indispensable, and I should go off and enjoy a well-earned weekend rest.

He was a kind man, but a strict disciplinarian, and I must admit that, to some degree, I lived in fear of him. If I was working on the bench filing a piece of metal in a vice, he would stand behind me, and the hairs on the back of my neck would stand up with apprehension. If I wasn't doing it right, he would push me aside and show me how it should be done. He was a man of the old school and had spent much of his life using hand tools. As a result, his forearms were more muscular than my legs, and the power he applied to the tool was scary. It was, however, a good lesson and a product of the apprenticeship system, where you learned on the job under valuable tutelage. He did, however, have a most kind heart, and his bark was certainly worse than his bite. When the New Year holiday came around, he would put his hand in his pocket and give me a bonus, at his expense, for a year's work well done. It is hard to imagine such an event happening today.

As an apprentice, you not only learned a trade, but also learned how to operate as a member of a team. The team leader and foreman was a first-class man called Jimmy Crawford, who had served in the war, and he taught me a lot, not only in terms of engineering but how to lead a team and get the best out of them. He led from the front, and no task was too humble for him. He approached his work with great enthusiasm and humor, and his leadership was inspiring. Later in life, when I was called upon to lead teams, I would cast my mind back to those apprenticeship days and try to emulate both Adam and Jimmy and lead from the front.

At the end of my apprenticeship, I still longed to become a police officer, but I decided to put that off for a while and to give something back to society and joined my father, who at that time was working in the Hull Institute for the Blind. I spent a year working alongside people who were semi-sighted or completely blind and, in some cases, were both blind and deaf. This was a humbling experience for me as a young man to have the privilege of working with these brave people who not only worked hard to overcome their disability but did so in such a cheery and graceful manner. I learned to communicate with those who were deaf and blind by using a special form of sign language, which involved using each other's hands to make signs. It wasn't easy to learn, but anything too easy isn't really worth the effort, and the pleasure that I was able to bring to them made the effort very much worthwhile. At the end of a year, my father took ill and died shortly thereafter in late 1963, so I took this as a sign that it was time for me to follow my dream and become a police officer.

Wherever they are in the world, Hawick folk tend to get in touch and stay in touch with other Hawick folk. As soon as I moved to Hull, I got in touch with Greg Ballantyne, whom I had known all my life and who was now a professional Rugby League player with Hull Kingstone Rovers. As a keen rugby fan, I spent many weekends watching Hull Kingston Rovers play, and after the match would join Greg and his girlfriend for a drink. In time they decided to get married, and Greg asked me to be his best man, and of course, I immediately agreed.

The wedding photo with me as the best man

The Police Years

As I was at that time living in Hull, I decided to apply to join the East Riding of Yorkshire Constabulary and am pleased to say that in spite of my lack of O and A levels (I left school at the age of 15 with no educational qualifications) my application was successful. In no time at all, I was off to the North East District Police Training School at Newby Wiske Hall in North Yorkshire. The training course was residential and three months long, and I must say that they worked us jolly hard. It was up to an early start and after a communal breakfast where we sat at long tables with benches, we moved on to classrooms, where we were taught the various elements of police law, practice and procedure interspersed with marching and physical training sessions, and twice a week at 6 a.m., we were bussed to the local public baths where we were trained in life saving. I was always a keen swimmer and found it no great hardship, but those who were non-swimmers or poor swimmers really struggled to make the grade. In the early sessions, we were required to build up water fitness by swimming countless lengths of the pool, and every time poor swimmers became tired and held on to the side of the pool, the instructor would come along and stand on their fingers and tell them in no uncertain terms to get back to it. At the end of the training course, we all qualified as lifesavers to a greater or lesser degree, and I am pleased to say that as an accomplished swimmer, I managed to qualify with a Bronze Cross, Bronze Medallion and Award of Merit.

I shared a dormitory with three students from Newcastle who had broad Newcastle or Geordie accents, and it took me some time to understand what they were saying. For example, one of them said to me, "come on wur gan for wur bait." It was then explained that he meant that we were going for our meal! On another occasion, when I asked where Mick was, they said he was at the "nettie." It turned out that a "nettie" was the word for a toilet in Geordie, and even more confusing, they sometimes called it the Mario, which was rhyming slang based on the great American racing driver Mario Andretti, which rhymes with "nettie." However, we four soon became good mates, and we were happy to assist each other with homework and the like.

There was little free time on the training course as the evenings were spent brushing up on police law and practical exercises. We did, however, find some time to relax, and our evening discussions in the bar were always lively and formed part of our bonding as a group.

Once again, I met a man who was to play a decisive part in my outlook on life. Each batch of recruits was divided into syndicates, and each syndicate had a sergeant who was the instructor in general police law and your mentor. I was lucky enough to have Sergeant Fred Purser as my syndicate instructor, and he was a giant of a man, not so much in stature but in character. He was from the northeast, had a strong northeastern accent and was quiet and non-assuming. His direct low-key approach to us as students was exceptional, and we all flourished under his tutelage and leadership. It happened that he was an expert in martial arts and had black belts at several dan levels in various disciplines. On occasions when he found time to join our evening discussions, he would tell us about his approach to police work and how he found that the low-key approach to policing paid dividends. His enthusiasm for police work was infectious, and these non-official sessions were probably more important than the official classroom sessions. He could happily use the low-key approach as he was a man who could look after himself when trouble broke out. He didn't need to strut the stage in his police uniform, and it was typical of him that he never boasted of his abilities. We did, however, learn from his colleagues on the directing staff how he was once called to a serious disturbance and managed to bring order to the situation and arrest several thugs on his own, not using a police truncheon but with his bare hands and martial art skills. His leadership and training paid off, and I managed to finish the course as the top student which was a great start to my police career and was very much a marker in my life!

Towards the end of my course, the training school had a cross-country race, and as I was not much of a runner (I was a slow-moving prop forward on the rugby field), I was delegated with a few others to venture out on the public roads in full uniform to direct traffic when the runners crossed the road. I remember feeling a great sense of occasion as it was the first time in my life, I was to appear in public in uniform doing actual police work rather than the staged practical exercises on the course. A small beginning but it does serve to illustrate to some degree the pride we developed in the police service.

My syndicate at the training centre – Fred Purser is in the middle of the front row and I am in the middle of the back row

My Official Police Photo

With the course completed it was time to return to my police force to begin my duties, and I was posted to the small seaside town of Hornsea in East Yorkshire, where I was put into the care of an experienced police constable who would show me the ropes. He taught me much, and perhaps the most important lesson he gave me was that the sight of the police uniform would do much of the work. Like Fred Purser, he stressed that a low-key approach was paramount and that there were two ways of handling any incident, the easy way and the hard way. The secret was to start with the easy way (i.e., the low-key approach), and if that failed, then and only then, to take the hard approach. This was in the days of the old big copper pennies, and he advised that when going into a situation that could turn violent, one should hold about six of these old pennies in your left hand, and if someone was about to turn violent to open your left hand letting the pennies drop on to the floor thus diverting the potential bad man's attention and providing you with the element of surprise in dealing with him physically. I hasten to add that in those days we had no radios, and help was not about to come sweeping around the corner like the guys with the white hats in the cowboy movies; it was always going to be up to you and you alone to deal with whatever situation presented itself.

The two weeks I spent in his care were all too short, and soon it was decided that I would have to stand on my own two feet and work shifts on the streets. This was a small town with a team of about six officers under the command of a sergeant. I remember starting my first night duty coming in to work at 11 p.m., knowing that I was the only police officer on duty in a radius of some 20 miles. Scary stuff, as unlike working in a big city force where you had backup, you were on your own and whatever happened, you had to deal with it. We worked what was called a "point" system, whereby every hour on the hour you would be required to be at a particular point in the town, usually at a public telephone box, so that if headquarters needed to contact you, they could do so by ringing the public phone box number.

Police work has long been a favorite subject for novel writers and drama series on television. Some portray a degree of realism and reality but many stray too far from the truth, perhaps as a means of producing a work that will be attractive to readers or viewers. As a result, the general public very often have an uninformed and even twisted view of the true role of the police service and the men and women who staff it. I always took the view that the Police Service was just that, a service to the public in the area of policing. Perhaps it is worth referring to the definition of a police constable that I was required to learn by rote more than 60 years ago and which is still close to my heart. "A constable is a citizen, locally appointed, but having authority under the Crown for the protection of life and property, the maintenance of order and the prosecution of offenders against the peace." I believe it is not by accident that reference is first made to protecting life and property and maintaining order and that the prosecution of offenders comes last. It is all too often the case that members of the public regard the true role of the police as prosecuting them for traffic offences and the like. That view was certainly common in my time as a police officer, and I suspect not too different today.

It is a truism that the main element of our work day or night was indeed the protection of life and property and good order. Where does the public turn when they encounter problems in their life but to the police? Missing persons, sudden deaths, thefts, road traffic accidents, floods and other natural disasters spring to mind as occurrences where police assistance is required. Dealing with the carnage of a road traffic accident in the middle of a winter night with cold gales blowing and snow falling; when waiting for an ambulance to come, standing in a ditch in two feet of freezing water supporting a seriously injured car passenger who was lying half in and half out of a vehicle with a serious back injury may seem like fiction, but believe me, it can be fact and I have dealt with such a situation. I am pleased to say that in that case the car passenger, a teenage girl, did survive and went on to live a full life in spite of her injuries.

The excitement of high-speed car chases as portrayed in TV dramas were not part of my everyday life and my early days as a police officer largely involved routine work which was totally unexceptional. Out in all weathers pounding the beat, day and night, was the rule. In daytime you were taught to walk on the outside of the pavement clearly visible to the general public, but at night you kept to the inside of the pavement with a blackened badge on one's helmet in order to provide as low a profile as possible. I suspect that when I joined the police service, I had expectations of leading an exciting life involving car chases and the like but as time went on, I very much regarded beat work as the most self-rewarding. You got to know your beat, to know who the good guys were and who the bad guys were. You had to learn every back lane and in a rural area the layouts of forests and woodlands. If you were good at your job, you became a walking encyclopedia of the area and could use that knowledge to be a better police officer. The vast majority of us did not have access to police vehicles but made our way on foot or on a bicycle, thereby allowing us the maximum level of contact with the public. It was always my view that the public were reassured by the sight of a uniformed police presence on the streets and although it is difficult to quantify, that visibility on the street no doubt played a role in the prevention of crime. There are valid arguments that the paucity of patrol vehicles and the total lack of radios led to inefficiency but there are opposite and, in my view, equally compelling arguments that the intimate level of contact uniform officers enjoyed with the public offset that notion of inefficiency.

Life in a county force was extremely different from life in a city or metropolitan force. Perhaps the most obvious difference was the lack of immediate backup by specialized officers, with the result that with the exception of really serious crimes each and every incident that you encountered would be dealt with by you from start to finish. As a result, an officer in a county force was obliged to develop a wider knowledge of police work, and with that came an enhanced sense of satisfaction. A sudden death was not immediately handed over to a Coroner's Officer for action, but each and every county officer was obliged to act as a Coroner's Officer, including attending post-mortem examinations and arranging an inquest if the coroner deemed it necessary.

This was one area that did not easily fit into the uninformed view of police work; dealing with sudden deaths and breaking the news of death to relatives was not something you were trained to deal with at training school but rather had to be learned on the job. It was my policy never to pass on death messages by phone but to deliver the news in person, breaking the news gently and helping the recipient to get over the shock. I remember having to break the news to a young girl of twenty years who had only been married two weeks that her husband had been killed in a traffic accident. She was alone at home and was understandably distraught. Once I managed to move her on from the initial shock, I got her to make a pot of tea whilst I contacted her parents who came to my assistance. I was relieved when they arrived but carried her grief with me for some time. It was however necessary to leave this element of the work at the office and not to bring it home and dwell upon it.

When acting as the Coroner's Officer in cases of sudden or violent death, you were obliged to ensure continuity of evidence for your report to the coroner by attending post-mortem examinations. I remember attending my first post-mortem examination with a considerable degree of trepidation. The seasoned officer I was understudying informed the pathologist that this was my first post-mortem examination. The pathologist said that if I was going to faint, I should do so backwards and not fall forward over the body! He was a pipe smoker and produced a pipe with a large bowl filled to the brim with tobacco. He handed me a box of matches, saying that my one and only role in the post mortem was to ensure that his pipe was kept lit. He was clever enough to tell me what he was doing at each and every stage, even to the extent of pointing out a clot in the heart of the deceased. He made it so interesting that when it was over, I realised that I had forgotten to feel queasy.

There were, however lighter moments, and I remember during a serious flu epidemic, we were dealing with sudden deaths daily. The mortuary at the local hospital was swamped, and on one particular day, we had so many post-mortem examinations that we were obliged to have a quick sandwich for lunch in the mortuary. The mortuary attendant took great pride in his domain, and it was his boast that his mortuary was so clean you could eat your dinner off the floor. The inevitable happened, and he dropped his sandwich, albeit in a napkin on the floor, and there was a pregnant silence when we all looked at him with anticipation. To his credit, he picked it up and ate it without skipping a beat, much to our merriment.

Another difference between a county force and a city force was the requirement for country officers to move location every two or three years. Married officers were provided with accommodation, but single officers had to find suitable lodgings. After my initial two years in the small seaside town, I was posted to Cottingham, which is one of several claimants for the title of the largest village in England. I was lucky in that the police force identified a suitable lodging for me that I shared with another single police officer. Indeed, this particular landlady had a succession of young police officers staying over a period of many years. She was used to our weird work hours as we worked a three-shift system. She was like a mother to us young officers and ensured we were well fed and watered. Fortunately, there was an excellent pub less than 100 yards from her house, and when we felt the need to get out from under her feet, and those of her husband and two teenage daughters, we could repair to the pub where we became part of the scenery.

Cottingham was once again a small operation where our presence was eight men under the supervision of a Sergeant. It was a very mixed police area being situated on the outskirts of the City of Kingston upon Hull and led onto green fields and farms. This mix provided us with a very varied professional life with criminal elements from the vast North Hull Council estate looking for easy pickings from the more affluent houses situated on the edge of the village. At the same time, we had to be well briefed on the regulations controlling the movement of farm animals, especially during outbreaks of foot and mouth disease and swine fever.

We had a good team, and it was a most enjoyable period of my police life. Once again, we deployed on pedal cycles and were rather envious of the Hull City Police Velocette LE motorcycles that were used by many beat men in the outer areas of the city. This water-cooled motorcycle with a small engine was actually quiet, but in stealth terms, no match for our trusty pedal cycles. We were not, in fact, provided with pedal cycles and were obliged to purchase our own, but the cost was offset by a pedal cycle allowance together with allowances for boots and torch batteries.

Around that time, our police force was undermanned, and we were obliged to work on many of our rest days, but on the brighter side, we were paid overtime for the extra days worked. It took some time to get used to shift work, and when we changed from mornings to afternoons and then to nights, we only had eight hours off between finishing one shift and starting the next. There was, however, the advantage that when we came off night shift, we enjoyed three days off, which was our monthly allowance of days off. Shift work was tiring as the body clock was continually having to adjust to the 0700-1500, then 1500 to 2300, and then 2300 to 0700 cycle. We did get sleepy, and I remember being told by an old-time officer that when making a "point" on a winter night in a telephone box, it was possible to snatch a few minutes of rest by leaning with one's back to the pay box with our truncheon in our hand. If we drifted off to sleep, then the truncheon would fall from our hand onto the concrete floor of the phone box, and the clatter would bring us back to instant alertness. Just being out of the extreme cold, snow and wind did, in fact, lead to sleepiness, and these short rest periods could be most welcome.

The truncheon fitted into a long pocket on the right-hand side of our uniform trousers and was so designed that when you were required to chase a suspect, the end of the truncheon banged against the back of your knee. So, all too often, you ran with the truncheon in your hand! Similarly, we carried a heavy pair of handcuffs that fitted into our left trouser pocket together with a first-field dressing, which was, I suppose, a throwback to the war, but did allow us the ability to apply it as a pressure bandage to stop bleeding when rendering first aid before the arrival of an ambulance which could take some time to come given the lack of instant communication in those days. The other two items of equipment we were obliged to carry were a warrant card, which identified us as a bona fide police officer, and a whistle, which could be used to attract attention. Looking back, it all seems so antiquated, but for the lonely police officer on his bicycle, these items were quite literally a lifeline.

However, in 1967 we witnessed the introduction of a personal radio that we could carry whilst on patrol. The initial radios were bulky and were carried strapped to our chests, and they had a four-foot-long aerial that was always getting in the way. Despite its bulk and difficulty of operation, it heralded in a new era whereby the lonely police officer on his cycle patrol could be directed to incidents, and perhaps more importantly, gave us a means of summoning assistance when needed. I am pleased to say that in time these early radios were replaced by a specially designed police radio manufactured by the Pye company, which had a small receiver that would clip onto our tunic and an equally small transmitter that nicely fitted into our pocket (both were actually smaller than the modern-day hand phones). This time the aerial was only four inches in length and these Pye pocket phones, as they were known, were efficient and easy to use and certainly revolutionized police work in general and in rural areas in particular.

It is perhaps hard to believe in these times of instant electronic communication that whenever we came on shift, we had to go through a hand-written journal that provided important information that we needed to be aware of whilst on patrol. Details of stolen vehicles, bank robberies, and other crimes had to be laboriously transcribed from the journal into our pocket notebook thereby providing us with an instant form of reference.

In those days, all our reports had to be laboriously typed by hand, and in time, we two-finger typists could get up a fair speed. The problem was that we were obliged to type most reports in triplicate and some in quadruplicate. So, when we made a mistake, we had to erase not only the mistake on the top sheet but also the mistake on the other copies. This was achieved by putting pieces of scrap paper between the carbon papers and the actual report paper so that the effect of using the eraser did not cause the carbon paper to put marks on the report underneath it. So far, so good, but there was a famous Chief Superintendent in the force who was a stickler for detail who insisted that after erasing each mistake, we had to use a pen knife to "polish" the surface of the paper in order that any evidence of the error was gone forever. All easier said than done, but in time, we did manage to comply with his edict, and it was not easy to see where we had been obliged to erase mistakes. Later, the force brought in proforma reports for simple traffic offences that we were allowed to complete by filling in the blanks using a ball pen. This was certainly much more efficient, and in later years, the force employed civilian typists who would type up our reports which we had dictated on a pocket tape recorder.

Life on the beat did have its lighter moments, and it is perhaps unsurprising that these humorous incidents all too often fail to find their way into TV police dramas. As I mentioned earlier, there was a need for a beat officer to communicate with all levels of society from the road sweeper to the Lord of the Manor. On one occasion, I was chatting to a working-class man, who was also a local town councilor, on crime trends when he said with an absolutely straight face, "They should bring back the birch – that was the best detergent that we ever had." I somehow managed to keep an equally straight face. On another occasion, I was interviewing a young woman in her home, and when I remarked how neat and clean her house was, she replied that this new Durex paint was wonderful – she did, in fact, mean Dulux Paint! Again, I just about managed to keep a straight face.

The rural part of Cottingham was home to many turkey farms, and in the run up to Christmas, when farm warehouses were full of turkeys, there was a need to carry out turkey anti-theft patrols. One of the parishioners was a man of some means, and he was one of many public-spirited members of the community who gave unpaid service by becoming a uniformed "Special Constable". He readily volunteered his services for the turkey patrols, and we patrolled together in uniform in his Rolls Royce motor car. Quite what members of the public must have made of this spectacle is hard to imagine, but I must say that I was happy to swap my bicycle for the warmth and comfort of his Rolls Royce on those winter nights, and we were certainly able to cover much more ground than I would have done on my bicycle.

When I first joined the police service, the experienced officer who was my mentor had two sayings that I carried with me throughout my police career. He maintained that rain was the best police officer and that a good policeman never got wet. It may seem to some that the "cup of tea" spots that a beat officer soon identified were a symptom of a dereliction of duty, but in fact, nothing could be further from the truth. These cup-of-tea sessions allowed us to bond with our community, and a surprising amount of intelligence could be obtained in the course of a cup of tea. Indeed, many citizens looked forward to a visit by the friendly local policeman, especially those who by reason of their occupation, were at some risk. The attendants at all-night filling stations were a case in point. They worked through the night alone and, in many cases, were genuinely afraid that they could become the subject of crime. I remember one such attendant who welcomed my visits and agreed to pay the price by noting down the registration numbers of all vehicles that visited his filling station between 1 a.m. and 5 a.m. I would collect these details from him before going off night shift and would pass them on to CID as many of these users of the filling station during the wee small hours were up to no good, and they appreciated this small but important piece of criminal intelligence. Members of the public are usually shy to pass on information to the police, probably because they do not want to become involved with authority, but are prepared to share information with a police officer who has taken the trouble to get to know them and in whom they have a degree of trust. So it is without shame that I admit to having more than my fair share of cup-of-tea spots on my beat.

Another lesson that I learned from him early on was that you never really know whom you are dealing with. This came home to me when on patrol on a winter's evening, I came across a Rolls Royce motor car parked illegally on double yellow lines outside a fashionable Italian restaurant. I did, in fact, know the owner of the restaurant and discreetly asked him if the owner of the car was in his restaurant. Within a couple of minutes, a well-spoken elderly gentleman came out of the restaurant, and when he admitted that it was his vehicle, I asked if he would be kind enough to move it a short distance to a parking space. This he happily did, and I told him that I intended to give him an official caution for his parking offence. I should have twigged when I asked for his license and other details, and he revealed that he lived in a large manor house and that he was someone of importance. In time, when the sergeant read my caution report, he informed me that the gentleman concerned was a member of the police committee. (To my shame, I should have known him to be so.) My colleagues were beside themselves with laughter, commenting that I would be in hot water for not knowing who he was and actually dragging him out of a restaurant for a minor offence. However, their merriment was cut short when the Chief Constable called me personally to inform me that this member of the police committee had told him of the incident and had commented that the young officer who dealt with him was most polite and courteous and should be commended for his action!

I must say that I found the official caution a valuable tool in dealing with minor road traffic offences. It enabled one to get the message across to a member of the public without the need for them to be prosecuted for a minor breach. The matter was dealt with, and they were happy to receive a caution rather than a prosecution and, in many cases, they were probably better members of the public for it. It also helped to dispel the myth that all police officers were lurking in the shadows waiting to catch motorists speeding and the like in order to accumulate numbers of prosecutions. The rules of the road had to be obeyed, but as a police officer, I had the authority to apply them in a fair and equitable way, and in the case of minor lapses, the caution was probably a better weapon than a summons. That said, blatant breaches of the law did deserve official action, and I was all too ready to report the offender for prosecution when it was appropriate.

Some cases went to court with the defendant pleading not guilty. At the police training school, we were taught how to give evidence in court but even so it could be a scary experience at least in the beginning. This was especially so when cases went to the Quarter Sessions or Assize Court for trial by jury where a smart barrister was all too ready to attack the evidence of a police officer in order to achieve a not guilty verdict for his client. Intimidating at first but with experience one realised that in many cases the defense barrister would attack the evidence of the police officer when his client had no other defense to the charge. In one such case when I was giving evidence, I took out my official police notebook to refer to a point of detail. The defense barrister asked what I was referring to and I explained that it was my official notebook. He asked whether the notes I was referring to were made at the time in question or whether I had made the notes at a later time in collusion with other officers. When I assured him that the notes were made at the time, he asked to see my pocket notebook. I handed the book to the clerk of the court who handed it to the defense barrister. I should explain that the police helmet is scientifically designed so that when it is raining the drops of water fall from the front of the helmet onto the page of the pocket notebook when you are writing notes. It was indeed raining when I made the notes and that page in the book was covered with splodges as the ink ran due to the rain drops. The defense barrister opened my notebook and just as quickly closed it again and handed it back to the Clerk of the Court. Seeing this the Judge asked if he could have a look at my notebook and when it was duly handed to him by the Clerk of the Court, he looked at it and said to the barrister that he no doubt would not wish to pursue the question of when the notes were made. The defense barrister smiled and agreed with the Judge. Many years later when I was a student studying law at university this very same defense barrister was a part time lecturer at my university and over a drink in the university bar after his lecture, he recalled the incident and described that when he opened the book his heart sank and that was compounded when the Judge asked to see the book. We became close friends.

After two years of beat patrolling in Cottingham, I was transferred to the Divisional Headquarters in Hessle, where I assumed the duties of Divisional motorcyclist. This was a wonderful job which entailed me being paid to ride a fast motorcycle, especially as I had been a keen motorcyclist from the age of 16. However, my thoughts that I was a good motorcyclist were put to the sword when I had to attend an advanced police motorcyclist course. There were three of us attending the course, which began with us being taught the theory of advanced motorcycling, including having to pass a written exam on that subject and the theory of two-stroke and four-stroke engines. However, once we got the theory out of the way, we were able to enjoy the practical side of the course, which entailed three trainees going out on the road with an experienced instructor. Initially, he would take the lead, and we students, in turn, would eventually be called on to take the lead, with him following on our heels. He would then criticise our riding style and teach us the finer points of positioning the bike in the right place on the road, at the right speed, with the right gear engaged, in order that we could ride the bike at high speed in a safe manner.

I later did the same course for advanced car driving, but that failed to match the excitement of the motorcycle course. The instructor for my motor car course was a stickler and always had a wooden ruler in his hand, and when I put my thumbs through the spokes of the steering wheel, he would whack me on the hands. I soon learned not to do it and to keep my thumbs on the actual wheel and not through the spokes. Like the motorcycle course, the car course commenced with learning the theory of mechanics and the Highway Code. Once we moved on to the practical driving part of the course, we were obliged to provide a commentary on our driving as we went along. In other words, we had to say out loud what we were thinking of doing as we drove along. This was difficult at first, but we soon got the hang of it. The advantage for the instructor was that our commentary, in effect, spelt out to him what we were thinking, which would serve to provide him with good feedback on how we were actually progressing and whether we were sticking to the theory provided in the police driving manual called Roadcraft. On one occasion, there was a child playing on the pavement but close to the road, and in my commentary, I meant to say that I was keeping my vehicle close to the middle of the road, thereby avoiding any danger to the child. As I did my commentary, the words, "child and kiddy" went through my brain, and I ended up saying that I was avoiding any danger to the "chiddy." He roared with laughter, and for many years, whenever I met with him, he would ask whether I had avoided any chiddies of late!

The police driving manual was, in effect, our bible, and we learned its content by heart. It was designed to ensure that we could not only drive well but were able to minimize the dangers that we might face on the road, especially when we were responding fast to a 999 call. In essence, the manual aimed that we should always be on the right place on the road, at the right speed, and with the right gear engaged, and to be in a position to respond safely to any danger arising from what we could see, what we couldn't see, and the possible circumstances that might reasonably be expected to develop. Yes, the last sentence is verbatim from the manual, which serves to demonstrate the degree to which we knew the manual, from cover to cover, which has enabled me to quote from it, word for word, after 60 years have passed. Speaking of gears, I remember the first day of our practical driving, and to my acute disappointment, there was not a shiny fast patrol car waiting for me but an old police Land Rover. We set out on a quiet stretch of road going from first to second, to third, and then to fourth gear, and back through the gears to first gear. The Land Rover had what was called a crash box and did not have synchromesh gears, which meant that we were obliged to double declutch both when changing up and down the gearbox. After a few hours of this, my left leg ached with the constant use of the clutch, but it was undoubtedly a lesson well learned.

Divisional motorcyclist was an extremely varied job as it involved not only dealing with road traffic accidents but also as a first responder to 999 calls throughout the Division. A fast motorcycle allowed you to get to the scene of an incident in quick time and in most cases, arrive before the traffic patrol cars, but the drawback was the weather. In summer, it was a joy, but in winter, it was a challenge due to inclement weather. When the weather got too bad, and the roads were icy, we stood down from motorcycle patrol and spent the rest of the shift as a passenger in a traffic patrol car. Getting into a warm patrol car after hours of riding around in extreme cold was extremely sleep making, and often it was not too long before you fell asleep, much to the merriment of your colleagues. I recall one occasion when working nights, the weather turned foggy, and I was ordered to return to headquarters and join the crew in a traffic patrol car. As the night went on the fog got even worse, and we were ordered to stand by off the road waiting to respond to any emergency. The inevitable happened, and we drifted off to sleep. When we woke, the fog had cleared, and there were two members of the public giggling at the sight of police officers fast asleep in a marked patrol car.

We were, of course, kitted out with sensible uniform clothing for motorcycling, including jodhpurs and knee-high leather boots, but the cold did penetrate, and I well remember on occasions arriving at the scene of an incident, and my hands were so cold that I was unable to write until I had warmed them up by putting them close to the hot cylinders of the motorcycle. The discomfort of winter motorcycling was offset by the bliss of working the night shift in the summer and coming out of the police station after supper at 3.30 a.m. when it was just breaking daylight and riding around the uncluttered highways and byways of the county free as a bird. There were other perks, and one of my duties was to deal with traffic attending motorcycle and car speed record attempts at RAF Elvington Airfield, which was a disused WW2 aerodrome with a runway over 3 kilometers long. This was a wonderful day out for a motorcycle enthusiast like me, being able to mingle with aficionados from all over the UK with a few from mainland Europe thrown in. Elvington was the venue for the setting of many records.

Indeed, on 3 October 1970, Tony Densham, driving the Ford-powered "Commuter" dragster, set the Official outright wheel-driven record at Elvington, averaging 207.6 mph (334.1 km/h) over the Flying Kilometer course. This broke Malcolm Campbell's record set 43 years previously at Pendine Sands. In the summer of 1998, Colin Fallows bettered Richard Noble's outright UK Record in his "Vampire" jet dragster at 269 mph (433 km/h) at Elvington. On 20 September 2006, Elvington Airfield was the location of a serious crash involving the Top Gear presenter Richard Hammond. The jet-powered car he was driving crashed at 280 mph (450 km/h). Hammond received serious brain injuries but made a full recovery.

These old WW2 aerodromes were in constant use for a variety of purposes, including test flying. They proved to be a boon when the Buccaneer aircraft was under development by the Hawker Siddeley Company at its factory in Brough in the East Riding of Yorkshire. Brough was another old WW2 aerodrome, but its use for flight purposes was cut short when the runway was declared to be too short for modern aircraft, given their speed. The result was that the prototype Buccaneers built at the factory had to be taken by road to another old WW2 aerodrome at Home-on-Spalding Moor for their maiden flights. Prior to this, the country surveyor and Hawker officials checked the route and many telegraph poles and road signs had to be moved away from the roadway, and narrow bridges widened to allow the safe passage of the towed aircraft. The aircraft were initially crated up for security reasons and were towed slowly the 20 miles to Home-on-Spalding Moor under police escort. This was a popular assignment for me as divisional motorcyclist. The day started with a very early Sunday morning breakfast at the factory, after which we escorted the convoy to its destination, ensuring the aircraft arrived without incident. Thus, it was that an aircraft capable of speeds of over 1000 kilometers an hour started its life crawling along country roads – unbelievable but true!

My next assignment was to what was called a rural beat where an officer was in charge of a series of villages, based at a police house that doubled as a police station, with 24-hour responsibility. I was fortunate as my rural beat consisted of the villages of Fulford, Heslington and Naburn on the outskirts of York. Fulford had an international-class golf course and was home to Imphal Barracks, which was the headquarters of the British Army's 15th Infantry Brigade. Heslington was an old medieval village that was transformed when it became home of the University of York. Heslington Hall, which was built in 1568, became the administrative headquarters of the university and the surrounding area was developed during and after my tenure into a series of eight colleges. Naburn was predominantly an agricultural community but was the site of the Naburn Psychiatric Hospital adjacent to the Fulford Maternity Hospital. My beat also included an 8-mile stretch of the river Ouse. Life was never dull with this mixed population of military men, university students, and doctors and nurses from the hospitals.

The establishment of Rural Beat officers was a catalyst in improving police and public relations. Each rural beat officer got to know his parishioners well, and vice versa and this interaction allowed the officer to serve the community better. For example, I had an arrangement with the Vicar of St Oswald's Church in Fulford whereby he gave me a sum of money from church funds, and when members of the community approached him for financial assistance, he would tell them that he was happy to assist but that they would be obliged to visit the local police officer who had authority to disburse funds on behalf of the church. We both were of the opinion that genuinely deserving cases who sought his help would be happy to receive the funds from the local police officer, and those not so deserving might well be put off. To my knowledge, the powers that be in the police force knew nothing of our arrangement, but it worked well, and sometimes it is necessary to apply police powers with imagination.

In 1968 the East Riding Constabulary was part of an amalgamation whereby the East Riding and North Riding Constabularies were merged with the City of York Police, with the new force being named York and North East Yorkshire Police. As a result, I was often called upon to perform duties in the City of York in addition to my own beat. This was an interesting experience as it allowed me first-hand to experience the role of a city officer and compare it to that of a county officer. Inevitably, they tended to see us as country bumpkins, and we regarded them as "uniform carriers." Neither term was accurate, and in time, we learned from each other and built-up trust and cooperation. One aspect of this new life that I did enjoy was the opportunity to take part in a new scheme whereby on a Friday and Saturday nights, about eight of us patrolled the city in a personnel carrier whereby we were able to turn up in numbers to deal with serious incidents and public disorder. It was a far cry from my early days when I was a lone officer with no assistance in a radius of 20 miles. The change also allowed me to gain insight into specialist departments such as CID and the force training department.

Being a strong swimmer and qualified lifesaver, I was invited to join the part-time sub-aqua unit that the new force had. We were a small force with limited funds, and we even made our own wet suits to save cost. This was not the type of diving that one reads about in travel brochures, where the water is warm and clear, and the reefs abound with exotic fish. Many of our assignments involved diving in dirty water with little visibility, searching for bodies or evidence, including murder weapons. In summer, it wasn't so bad, but in winter, we were often obliged to break the ice before diving into freezing water. Nowadays, most police forces provide dry suits for their dive section, but our wet suits flooded immediately upon insertion into the freezing water, which resulted in an instant drop in body temperature and a searing pain across the forehead. However, after time the film of water between the wet suit and the body warmed up from body heat and provided a degree of insulation. Slowly swimming along the bottom of the river Ouse using our hands to attempt to locate a body in three feet of mud is hardly glamorous, but it was a job that had to be done, and we were volunteers! It was necessary to retain a high standard of "water fitness" and our training dives involved swimming against the current in the river Ouse until we could no longer make progress. At the end of these training dives, we scrambled out of the water, unable to stand with our legs quivering, but the camaraderie of the group kept us going, and the level of fitness we achieved ensured our safety when the going got tough on operational dives. These training dives also provided a degree of interest for the many tourists who flocked to York in the summertime. However, in the summer months, we would occasionally go off to the seaside where we were able to perform what were called open-water dives and swim through the forests of seaweed that were up to 100 meters deep and as tall as trees. We combined these open water dives with running a safety course on the beach for children on the safe use of snorkels!

Me (King Neptune) with a farm implement found in a pond that we were searching for proceeds of a crime

Our Headquarters in York were shared with the York Fire Brigade with the result that both services developed a close bond but also a degree of rivalry. We had a shared canteen, and much amusement was had when the fire alarm bells went off, and all the firemen eating their meal had to drop their knives and forks and shoot down the sliding pole to their awaiting fire engines. The last man down the pole usually missed the departure of the engine, and he had to gather up the plates of food left by his colleagues and put them in a relatively cool oven to keep warm for their return. If the fire was a big one and they were out for a long time, they either had to accept that they had missed their meal or struggle through the remains of their meal, which by that time had probably become tainted by bacteria. Policemen and firemen were natural allies, and strong friendships were developed. Likewise, we developed strong bonds with nurses who staffed the local hospital A & E unit. The nurses got to know us well as we had often to escort the ambulance to the hospital and then liaise with the hospital staff regarding the identity of the injured and details of their next of kin. I recall one incident when I was Divisional motorcyclist where I was run down by a speeding motorist at the scene of a traffic accident and had to be taken to the hospital by ambulance to have a wound to my leg attended to. Once my leg was stitched up, the nurses took great delight in wheeling me around the hospital in a wheelchair in police uniform minus my trousers!

The local hospital could also become a favorite spot for a cup of tea, and many of us were regular visitors. On one occasion, when I was supervising a young newly joined officer, we called at the local hospital, and I left him in the car when I went to the porter's lodge to pick up the key to the mortuary. After I opened up the mortuary, I said I would put the kettle on and asked him to get the milk out of one of the huge fridges. He duly opened a fridge and was shocked when faced with rows of bare feet of the bodies lying on trays.

Having passed my Sergeant's and Inspector's exams with flying colors, I was happy to assist the force training department and I volunteered to improve the training of Special Constables in my own time. My efforts came to the attention of the Chief Constable, who decided that I should go off to the Home Office Central Planning Unit at Ryton on Dunsmore near Coventry to train as a lecturer in police law. This was a thoroughly enjoyable course where we were trained in advanced methods of teaching police law, and although I was a mere constable in a class of sergeants and inspectors, I managed to come top of the course. Needless to say, the Chief Constable was delighted that I had lived up to his assessment and I was immediately posted to the Force Residential Training School at Solberge Hall in North Yorkshire.

The school catered for all the training needs of the force, and I quickly got into the role of preparing and delivering lectures on the constantly changing police and criminal law. It was an exacting time and our days were long as we kept our students working late into the night. It was, however, rewarding being in a position to pass on my knowledge to the students and to improve their understanding of the law and practice. It is often said that a lawyer's knowledge resides in his law books, but a police officer is obliged to carry his knowledge of the law in his head. Not for him the reference to the textbooks when faced with an incident, rather, he must act immediately in the heat of the situation and get it right! Our "bible" was a book entitled Moriarty's Police Law and we would constantly refer to it when writing up reports and preparing papers for court hearings. (Over the years, I would tell my daughter stories of my time as a police officer and how we used this book and some years ago, to my great pleasure and surprise, she presented me with a copy of the book, which was the version used by me as a young constable.)

I should point out in all due humility that following being the top student on my initial training course, I was also the top student on my first and second refresher course over the next two years, and I then spent much of my free time brushing up on police law in preparation for the nationwide Sergeants exam. I developed a method whereby I would read aloud from the law books and record my voice and then listen to these recordings to further enhance my studies whenever I had some time to spare. In the event, I passed the sergeants exam with such high marks that the Chief Constable summoned me to his office and suggested that I sit for the Inspectors exam the following year, and if I were to achieve a good result, he would wish to discuss further my career development. My performance in the Inspectors exam was such that I was summoned by the Chief Constable, who suggested that, given my knowledge of police law, I should apply to a university to study law.

University Life

At the time, there was a scheme to recruit graduates into the police force who would enjoy accelerated promotion to the senior ranks. He was of the opinion that there was no guarantee that these graduates would make good police officers. His preference was to identify officers who had proven their worth and ability and send them to university to obtain a degree. I replied that I was flattered to receive such an offer but doubted I would be selected for university as I had no O or A levels. He was of the opinion that this should not be a bar to university entry and advised that I should apply as a "mature student" and allow him to provide an appraisal to the university authorities. This was duly done, and despite my lack of formal educational qualifications, I was accepted by the University of Hull to study for a degree in law.

I went to university with a degree of trepidation as 14 years had passed since I left school without formal qualifications, and I was still unsure whether I would be academically able to cope. I must say that my initial meetings with my fellow students left me in no doubt as to the gap in our ages and backgrounds. I was keenly aware that being a serving police officer could be a handicap in building relations with my fellow students, and decided not to broadcast the fact. That said, the University Law Department was well aware of the fact that I was a serving police officer, as were most of the lecturers. There was one humorous occasion when, during a tutorial shortly after the course began, a young extremely anti-establishment female student was sounding off about the police and how they simply invented facts in order to prey upon innocent citizens. The lecturer laughed and asked whether he should tell her who I was or should I apprise her of the facts. I duly did so, and she was mortified, and although I could sense that she saw me as a devil complete with horns, we agreed to differ on many issues but nevertheless became good friends. Being a mature student had its challenges, and it took me some considerable time to shed the disciplined background of the police and fit into the laid-back life of an undergraduate. Needless to say, I found the criminal elements of the course easy enough to master, but some of the more philosophical aspects of law and comparative law were quite a challenge.

I well remember when the Dean of the Law Department, Professor Hugh Bevan, gave his opening address to our academic year, he asked us to look to the person on our right and left and be prepared for the fact that in a year they would perhaps no longer be there. He explained that the law was not for all and that it was normal for the law department to lose at least 25% of its students after the first year, they having decided that the discipline of studying law was not for them. I wondered whether I would be one of those who failed to last the course and determined that I would work hard to achieve success.

The social life at university was hectic, especially in the early months when the younger students were keen to let off steam, and the bars did a roaring trade. They welcomed the break from parental supervision with open arms and seemed determined to rebel both in terms of dress and behaviour, especially in the early part of the first year. However, as the year progressed, most of them got down to hard work, albeit a bit reluctantly, and as exams approached, their work effort became more and more pronounced. They arrived at morning lectures haggard from a night of feverish study, and still, they struggled to cope with the demands of the course. I had determined from the beginning to regard life at university as a job and worked studiously for 8 to 10 hours each and every day, 7 days a week, and a couple of days before exams, I would put the books away, working on the premise that if I didn't know it then I was unlikely to know it in 2 days' time. Therefore, I arrived in the examination room fresh from a couple of days of pure relaxation in a fit mind able to express my views on paper.

It was not always possible to put to the back of my mind the fact that I was a serving police officer. It was clear that the lecturers expected more from me as a mature student and were keen to have me express views that were perhaps different from my peers in tutorial classes. Without doubt, it broadened my view on life in general, and some, at least of my fellow students, were able to form a different opinion on the police. There were many extramural events that were great fun, and I was grateful for the opportunity to become a volunteer in a legal help group that the department ran, whereby we tried to advise poor citizens on a range of legal issues free of charge. My police background was certainly a plus and enabled me to play a full part in the group's activities.

Another aspect of university life that I enjoyed was taking part in moot courts. In a moot court the participants take part in a simulated court proceeding whereby a point of law is debated by the participants. It was certainly useful training for those students who intended to pursue a career at the bar, and in my case, I indeed found my experience giving evidence in both Quarter Sessions and Assize courts stood me in good stead and provided me with the confidence to put forward strong arguments. An unfair advantage maybe, but it was certainly an enjoyable experience, especially as, on many occasions, the "Judge" was one of several barristers who worked part-time at the University and with whom I had tangled in live court proceedings as a police officer! (The police pocketbook incident,)

At the end of the first year, my exam results were good, and I was able to go forward to year two. On the first day of the first term in the second year, I looked around in the lecture theatre, and it was certainly noticeable that the thinning out that our professor had forecasted had indeed taken place, and many familiar faces were absent. Some had decided that University was not for them and had left to pursue other paths and others had opted to change disciplines for whatever reason. For those of us who remained, our studies continued, and the workload became progressively tougher. My decision to work a steady 8-to-10-hour day was paying off, and I became more confident in my ability to last the course and obtain an honours degree. Life wasn't all a bed of roses, and there were occasions when my conservative views led to differences of opinion with a few lecturers. I remember that on one occasion, I had to write a dissertation on the alleged use of torture by the British Authorities in Northern Ireland. As my dissertation progressed, it soon became clear that my views clashed severely with the supervising lecturer, who was well known for his anti-establishment views. Our opposing views were well known, and to the credit of the department, it was decided that my dissertation should be double-marked with a second more establishment-minded lecturer carrying out the second marking. The system worked, and the mark I received for the work was fair and equitable.

Dissertations were challenging, but it was satisfying to be able to investigate a legal subject in some depth and prepare arguments on the legal points involved. Another dissertation I was obliged to write was on the legality in International Law of the "Unilateral Declaration of Independence" (UDI) of the Smith Government in Rhodesia. With my then limited knowledge of International Law and international affairs, I found it hard to understand the Smith position, and it wasn't until many years had passed and I visited Zimbabwe on British Government business, and saw the all too apparent results of years of Mugabe rule that I began to understand and have some sympathy for the actions taken by Smith. Rhodesia had been the bread basket of Africa, but after years of mismanagement, Zimbabwe could hardly manage to feed its own people.

I suppose that it was inevitable that with my police background, I would stand out, and it turned out that I stood out in a much wider sense than I had ever imagined. Indeed, interest was shown in me by barrister's chambers in London, who no doubt felt that a barrister with a police background would strengthen the criminal element of their chamber. I was flattered by their approach but made clear that it was my intention to return to the police service.

It was then suggested that I would have a good chance of passing the FCO recruitment tests but I was warned that the tests were extremely daunting but out of curiosity I decided to give it a go. As a result, I then started the vetting process, examining my life to ensure I measured up to expectations and I am pleased to report that I was successful and offered a career with the Foreign Service.

Foreign Service

It had always been my intention to return to the police service upon completing my degree, and this offer hit me with mixed feelings as I really enjoyed being a police officer, and with a good solid honor's degree in law, my police career was primed to take off. I arranged an interview with the new Chief Constable of my police force whom I had never met and whom I suspected had probably never heard of me. It was with a degree of trepidation that I attended the meeting not quite expecting how my new situation would be received.

I explained to the new Chief Constable the background that had led to me being sent to university by his predecessor and that I had been offered a position with the Foreign and Commonwealth Office (FCO). He smiled and said that he was already aware of the job offer as he had been consulted by the proposed new employers. I said that I was now somewhat embarrassed and unsure of what to do, as it had always been my intention to return to the police service after university. He made it clear that, in his opinion, the police service had not sent me to university, but rather I had been sent there at the expense of the ratepayers and taxpayers, and should I decide to go ahead and join the FCO, I would still be working for them. He then outlined how he saw my career in the police service should I choose to stay, which in all due humility, was mind-blowing but if I decided to go ahead and accept the offer, I could do so with his blessing, as he felt I would be an ambassador for the police service within Whitehall and I could certainly join them with his blessing. He added that if I did go ahead and found that life there was not for me, then I could return to the police service and renew what he felt would be a highly successful career as a senior police officer.

I then went on to complete my third year and received an LLB with honours.

My Graduation Photo

And so began what was to be a new chapter in my life and one which I am unable to discuss in any detail in this book due to the provisions of the Official Secrets Act. Suffice it to say that I did not return to the police service and I served in the Foreign Service for 25 years.

I must admit that I found life in the hallowed halls of Whitehall quite different from the police service, but I quickly settled down and found the new challenges to be stimulating. It was quite an experience to become involved in formal dinners where the after-dinner port had to be passed to the left! My social life was also vastly different from what I had experienced in Scotland and Yorkshire and I was obliged to fit into a completely different lifestyle.

One day I was sitting at my Whitehall desk when I received a call from my lifelong friend Jim Beattie who played in our Boys Brigade Pipe Band at the same time that I did and was in fact my next-door neighbor in the prefabs in Hawick. In the broad dialect of my hometown, he asked if it would be possible for me to take a few days leave the following week. I asked why and he said that the current Drum Major of the Hawick Pipe Band had fallen off a horse and broken his leg and the band was due to lead the Scottish contingent of the British Legion to the 60th anniversary of the Battle of the Somme in France. The question was whether I could take leave and, if so, would I be prepared to lead the band as Drum Major on the visit to France. The answer to both questions was yes, and it was agreed that they would pick me up by bus outside Madam Tussauds in Central London at 4 a.m. the following Tuesday morning and would bring the Drum Major's uniform with them. I waited outside the venue until almost 5 a.m., by which time I was convinced that it was all a hoax when around the corner came the bus.

The trip to France was a memorable one especially so as former soldiers from our hometown who had fought at the Somme were with us on the bus and stayed with us in France. It was an honor, and extremely humbling to listen to these old soldiers relate their experiences when they passed fields and, in some cases, point out where their comrades had been killed. The people of France took them to their hearts and looked after them in regal style. We played at a service at the Thiepval Memorial in Picardy, which is the largest British Battle Memorial in the world. Designed by Sir Edwin Lutyens, it has the names of 72,000 dead soldiers whose bodies were never found but lie buried in the mud of the Somme. It was a most humbling experience to lead the band's performance at the memorial, and it will live with me for the rest of my life.

Me leading the band at The Somme anniversary

We also visited the town of Albert, where the spire of the Basilica Notre Dame De Brebieres was badly damaged by shelling during the war. Atop the spire was the Virgin Mary holding Christ and the shelling knocked them almost to the horizontal. The folklore was that if the virgin and child did not fall then, Albert would prevail and would be liberated. In the event, it did not fall due to German efforts but later fell during an allied bombing of the town during the liberation of Europe.

Whilst we were there, the mayor of the town gave a reception and arranged for us to play around the town. A wedding was taking place in the town at the time and the mayor asked if we could do him and the town a great favor by playing into the wedding reception. Our approach was silent, and when we got to the venue, the double doors to the location were flung open, and we struck up the music and marched into the middle of the wedding reception. The bride, who knew nothing of our plans, was in tears of joy, and she had a wedding that no other bride in Albert is ever likely to equal. We also attended a reception given by the mayor at the town hall, and as I entered the upstairs room where the reception was being held, a breeze was blowing through the open windows. As a result, my plaid was flowing behind me in the wind, and a French lady was heard to remark in a loud voice, "Ah tres magnifique, mais tres formidable," much to the amusement of all concerned.

Posting to British High Commission, Singapore

After many months in Whitehall, I was posted overseas to work in our High Commission in Singapore, which was to begin a long and happy association with the Far East.

In front of the British High Commission, Singapore

Our home in Ridley Park, Singapore

As someone with no real experience of living overseas, it was fascinating to live and work in Singapore, where I could take in new cultures, religions, and food. The climate was hot, and it took some getting used to, as did the diplomatic life. There will be some who regard the diplomatic life as an easy number with privileges such as duty-free living and fancy houses. However, the fact is it is an extremely exacting and time-consuming career. We enjoyed a normal working day of around nine hours, but to have an evening off was the exception rather than the rule. Evenings were spent attending National Day cocktail parties and then on to a working dinner where the subject at the dinner table was politics. It sounds like a great life, but it is extremely tiring, and I now regard it as a great pleasure to be able to spend my evenings at home with my wife watching television and taking it easy.

Initially, it was quite difficult to settle down to life so far from home and childhood friends, but later, in the late 1990s, a group of young people from my hometown very much led by a childhood friend, Graham Peacock, and a few others, set up a group on the internet called the Teri Hub. This was long before Facebook and the like and proved to be a valuable tool for keeping in touch, especially for those of us who had left the town. Essentially, we all knew each other, and those who remained in the town ensured that those of us who were exiles were kept in touch with what was going on in the town. The hub ensured that our friendships blossomed, and even to this day many of us from the hub are still in touch through Facebook.

The seventies were a time of great transition in Singapore largely due to the foresight and vision of its Prime Minister Lee Kwan Yew, who led the country through its pioneer days to the successful and bustling economy it is today. Lee had confidence in his policies, but just as important, he had confidence in his people. His critics branded him as too controlling, but it was his steely conviction that ensured that Singapore would weather the storms of race relations, race riots and extremely dominant trade unions to become a well-run, efficient, and safe island state. He was intelligent and shrewd enough to hand pick a supporting reliable ministerial team in the early days, and that dedicated and very much hands-on team played a vital part in his success.

I had the pleasure of having an intimate dinner with him in 1977 when he stated that the way forward for Singapore at that time would involve three policy objectives. Firstly, he explained that wages in Singapore were too low, and he was determined to double them in four years. Secondly, he pointed out that Singapore was the world leader in the manufacture of black and white televisions, and his plan was to drop black and white televisions altogether and move on to concentrate on much higher technology fields. His final point was that although Singapore had a bright and hard-working population, he saw the need to retain expatriates in the workplace for at least the next 20 years. Not unexpectedly, all these three aims came true, and Singapore still retains a sizeable expatriate element in academia and business.

At the risk of boring readers, I would like to set out the principal elements in Singapore that struck me in my early days. Language can be a very emotive subject in any country and Prime Minister Lee said that the Singapore Government would have four official languages reflecting the racial mix of its people. Mandarin Chinese was perhaps an obvious choice as ethnic Chinese made up the vast majority of the people. The Singaporean Chinese originated from many different regions of China and by making Mandarin an official language he could gradually wean them away from their traditional use of dialects which he saw as potentially divisive and a barrier to national unity. The choice of Malay was a given as they made up the second biggest ethnic element and having their native tongue as one of the national languages would go far in healing the wounds caused by the race riots in the early period of his leadership. Tamil is the third national language and by granting it this status he could avoid the mistakes of the Solomon Bandaranaike Government in Sri Lanka (formerly Ceylon) when Bandaranaike ordained that the language of the civil service would be changed overnight from English to Sinhalese. It has been said, and I have no reason to disbelieve it, that when Singapore was granted its independence Lee stated that he hoped that one day Singapore would be as well run as Ceylon. One of the reasons for his view on Ceylon was that it had a superb civil service that almost entirely consisted of Tamils who were well educated and spoke good English in addition to their native tongue. The government decided in the 1950s that henceforth the only national language would be Sinhalese. By that stroke of the pen the Tamils who ran the civil service lost their jobs and livelihood as they did not have command of the Sinhalese language and their grievances over this issue smoldered on and eventually played their part in the formation of the Liberation Tigers of Tamil Eelam (LTTE) which brought so much strife and bloodshed to the country. Finally, Lee chose English as the fourth language probably as it had been the language of the Colonial Government but also because of its universal use in business and technology. It may seem strange, but all government documents are printed in the four languages and directions in the public transport system, for example, are set out in those languages.

Another feature that struck me was the sheer efficiency of the country, where common sense was paramount. The control of state land and the development of housing is an example of the forward-looking policies of the government. Satellite towns were introduced, and high-rise low-cost government apartment blocks were built by the Housing & Development Board (HDB). The working class of Singapore who had previously lived in simple wooden houses in villages (kampong) were able to move to modern apartments with social amenities on their doorstep. The planning of these new towns is a model for town planners in that these new towns all centered around a hub, and local government offices, shops, restaurants, and public transport were all situated in those hubs. As the policy developed, the modern and efficient mass Rapid Transport System (MRT) had stations in all the hubs, and the provision of feeder bus services to the MRT stations resulted in an excellent public transport system. The effect of this policy can be seen today as 90% of the population are owner occupiers, and 80% reside in these government-built flats. I should perhaps add that the first flats were rushed into service and whilst not substandard they were quite basic. However, as time went by, these older units were torn down and replaced by better quality and better-equipped estates.

In Singapore, taxation is relatively low, but all workers are obliged to pay 20% of their salary into what is called the Central Provident Fund (CPF), which is effectively a method of enforced savings. The employer also has to contribute 17%, and the government manages the use of these funds through carefully chosen investments, and the people can draw on these funds for the purchase of HDB flats and health provisions. An admirable system that works well both for the government and the people.

The Love of My Life

During my second year in Singapore, the High Commissioner asked if I could represent him at a charity event on the following Saturday afternoon. I immediately agreed but was somewhat taken aback when he explained that it was a charity fashion show organized by the Singapore Junior Chamber of Commerce. The thought of spending my Saturday afternoon at a charity fashion show hardly filled me with enthusiasm, but it was my duty to represent the High Commissioner.

So, there I was on a sunny Saturday afternoon in a shopping mall next door to the Istana which was the official residence of the President of Singapore, sitting with the joint chief guest the Russian Ambassador, his interpreter, and representatives of the Junior Chamber of Commerce. We sat on a raised stage area with the "catwalk" running out in front of us. Before the actual fashion show began, there were a series of plugs for the charity that the organizers were promoting during this preamble. During this time, I noticed that one of the fashion models was complaining about the arrangements for the show (I later learned that she was complaining that the changing rooms were overlooked by the spectators on the floor above). I was intrigued that this model was prepared to take issue or, should I more accurately say, harangue the organizers in the way that she did. I pointed this out to one of the organizers sitting next to me, and he said that the model in question was none other than Debra de Souza, a former Miss Singapore.

Anyway, the fashion show went off without incident, and I spent the next six months looking for Miss de Souza, but she was nowhere to be found. She wasn't on the diplomatic or nightclub circuits, but I saw her every day on the cover of women's magazines and the like. At that time, I had a good chum who was a Singaporean rugby player, and on Wednesday evenings, he and I would hold dinner parties at my official residence. One week he said that he knew a girl that I should meet and suggested that he bring her along to our next party. I said that I certainly didn't require him to find girls for me and I would choose my own company. He persisted and insisted, pointing out that this girl was just right for me, and in the end, to keep him quiet, I agreed to his suggestion. When we arrived at the girl's house to pick her up, who should walk out but the model from the fashion show wearing one of her fathers old-fashioned shirts, a black silk tie and a pair of black satin tight trousers complete with black high heeled shoes and a ponytail coming out of the side of her head. His judgement was spot on and as a result my six-month search for this model were brought to a happy end.

Miss Singapore 1973

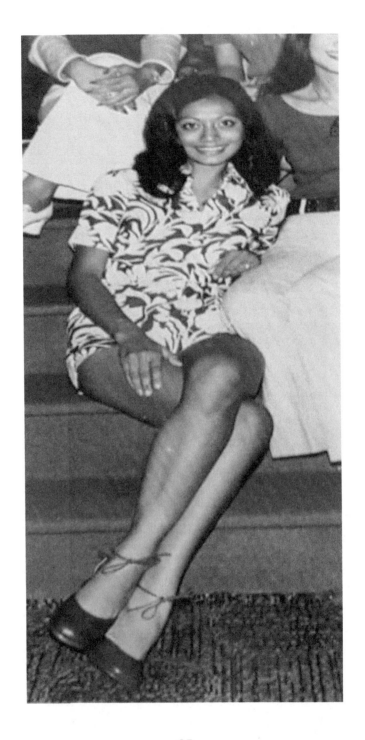

Debra on the first cover of Singapore's Female Magazine

I think these photos suffice to illustrate why I was so besotted with the model at the charity fashion show!

Within a year, we were married, and Debra started a new life as the wife of a diplomat with all that the role entailed.

However, after the wedding, we went off on a honeymoon which took us around the world in three months. It was fortunate that my work program was so busy in the preceding years that I had a lot of leave owing, and we took the opportunity to have a once-in-a-lifetime experience. Our honeymoon began in the honeymoon suite at the famous Raffles Hotel in Singapore, and we then travelled through Asia and Europe before ending up in Canada and the United States. In Canada, we were hosted by the Royal Canadian Mounted police, who were kindness itself and showed us around Ottawa and the Gatineau Park.

In the United States, we visited both the East and West coasts, and in California, where we were visiting Disneyland Park, Debra took the opportunity to meet up with her old friend Amanda Jones who represented USA in the Miss Universe Contest in 1973 in Athens when Debra represented Singapore.

We also took the opportunity to contact an old friend of mine, the American rally driver Brian Chuchua, in Anaheim. I first met Brian in 1977 when he was competing in the London to Sydney Marathon car rally. There were several British drivers taking part in the rally, which was due to come down the Malaysian Peninsula and into Singapore, where the teams would have a rest whilst their vehicles were shipped from Singapore to Perth in Australia. I, therefore, asked the High Commissioner whether the High Commission would be taking any measures to mark the presence of the British drivers. The High Commissioner said that he had no intention in involving the High Commission in the event, but if I felt so strongly, then I should do so on my own. I, therefore, went along to the official welcome for the drivers at the Hilton Hotel and introduced myself to the British drivers. We then went up to the rooftop bar at the hotel for drinks, and it occurred to me that I should, in fact, invite them all to come along to my home where they could enjoy British hospitality and duty-free drinks. They all agreed and began to get up to follow me, except one driver who seemed not keen to go. When I asked him why he said that he was in fact an American driver and had simply been in the company of a British driver in his team. I shook him by the hand and made clear that he was most welcome to join us, and he happily came along and spent the evening making merry at my place. The following day, I received a thank you note from him with an invitation to join him for dinner at a posh restaurant that evening. I went along and found that he was at the head of a table of many drivers. I had the impression that he was, in fact, hosting the meal and asked James Ingleby, a British Driver with the Jeep team, who was sitting next to me, whether we were really going to let him pay for the meal or should we all chip in. James laughed and said that I should not worry as Brian ran the biggest Jeep distributorship in California and could well afford to pay for the meal. At the end of the meal, I thanked Brian for hosting the dinner, and he said that if I should ever find myself in the US, I should contact him and he would arrange to fly me to his home in California in one of his many helicopters!

So, I duly telephoned his Anaheim Office, and the phone was answered by David Howes, another British driver in the 1977 Jeep team. He asked where we were and said that we should just stay there, and after a few minutes, he came around in a Jeep and picked all three of us up and took us to Brian's place. As I mentioned earlier, when I met Brian in 1977, he said that he had a warehouse full of helicopters and would be happy to fly us around. He took us into the warehouse which was indeed filled with many helicopters and he then asked Debra which helicopter she liked best, and she pointed out a neat little 2-seater. He then told them to get the helicopter ready, and he gave Debra and Amanda personal flights over the Disney complex. I must admit that when he told me in 1977 about the many helicopters he owned, I felt that he was embellishing the story, but it was true, and his hobby was to purchase helicopters that had suffered a hard landing and bring them back up to spec. Yet another example of dislocation of expectation in my life.

Diplomatic life involved a lot of travel, and the following year, we managed to spend some time in Hawick, so that Debra could experience her first Common Riding, which she thoroughly enjoyed.

Debra and I with Frank Scott, the Provost of Hawick

After the honeymoon, Debra was obliged to fit into the diplomatic life, but she did, however, manage to combine that with modelling, and I often went along to watch the shows. Our early married years worked out well as she would often be out and about on photo shoots and modelling assignments, and I would attend many diplomatic events on my own, thus saving her the prospect of attending diplomatic functions that could be boring, to say the least.

When I first went to Singapore, it had an outstanding International Airport at Paya Lebar, but such was the government foresight that it replaced this perfectly good airport with Changi International Airport, which is renowned worldwide for its efficiency and provision of services and has achieved many awards. With hindsight, Paya Lebar would probably not have been capable of dealing with the increase in air travel, and its expansion would no doubt blight local communities, but it was a bold but innovative move nevertheless.

The small land area of Singapore (the little red dot on the map, as former Indonesian President Habibie called it) was both a plus and a minus. On the plus side, the compact size made government activities such as the provision of postal services and the like infinitely more manageable than they would have been in a sprawling country such as Indonesia with its almost 18,000 islands ranging over several thousand kilometers. The downside was the scarcity of land, especially as the population grew, which led to land reclamation schemes which have allowed the country to grow its land area by more than 25% since the 1970s. It is perhaps typical of Singaporeans that the phrase little red dot, meant as a slight by Habibie, has been turned around and has become a badge of pride reflecting the successful development of Singapore despite its size.

Singapore is a multi-cultural country and as one would expect its choices of food reflect the cultural variations. When I arrived there, when free from evening diplomatic functions, I immediately adopted the Singapore habit of eating at food stalls, known locally as hawker centers. Here one could eat al fresco at well-designed and controlled, but above all, inexpensive food outlets. Chinese, Malay and Indian food was available, with many variations of each. Being new to the East, I was struck by the range of food on offer and was keen to try these exotic dishes, none of which I had tried before and most of which I had never even heard of. I must admit that initially, much of the food was too spicy for my European tastes, but before long, I was happy to eat local food and developed a taste for hot spicy curries and the like. The hawker centers provided a potpourri of both Singaporeans and tourists, and the excellence of the food was only bettered by the ambience of raucous hawkers vying for trade and the general hustle and bustle. Even though I often ate alone, the hawkers made you very welcome, and when it was really busy, it was a delight to enjoy the company of Singaporeans at the same table who were always ready to suggest that I should try their favorite dishes, most of which I washed down with excellent cold Singaporean Tiger beer. The formality of the diplomatic life was certainly offset by the new sights, sounds, and tastes of the east, and little did I realize then that Asia would become home to me.

I should hasten to add that the Singapore of 1977 was vastly different to the Singapore of today, with more than double the population and a whole new raft of public transport systems. The public transport system of modern Singapore is ambitious, clean, efficient and definitely fit for purpose. The ever-expanding MRT underground system is one of the most modern in the world, with air-conditioned driverless trains which provide efficient service at a very reasonable price. Its bus service has a modern fleet with routes that are designed to not only link different parts of the island but also designed to provide a feeder service from the outer fringes of the new towns to the central hub. Taxis are plentiful, and its modern fleet is well controlled by the government and now enhanced by hailing services such as Grab. There are many who would argue that the government of Singapore is a nanny state with overbearing controls, but when contrasted with other countries in the Asia Pacific Region, its uncorrupted and efficient government stands out as a beacon.

Anyway, enough of this travelogue in favor of Singapore and back to life on the ground. My day job kept me busy, but some evenings were free, and I used them to explore the highways and byways of Singapore. This became a regular activity at the commencement of a new overseas posting; it was like an artist looking at a blank canvas with a desire to fill it with color and life. It was an essential task as it was imperative as a diplomat to be able to find one's way around, but it was also a pleasure to explore just what made each capital city tick. It was also a good way to make friends amongst the local community outside the rather sterile diplomatic community. I remember a colleague who, on an overseas posting, visited a local carpet seller two or three times a month to bargain with the owner over a particular Persian carpet that caught his eye. As time went on, the bargaining took place over coffee, and in time, they became close friends, and the bargaining gave way to friendly chat on life in that city, making comparisons between life there and the UK. In the end, he never bought the carpet, but made a lifelong friend!

Having come from a background where fixed price was the norm, it was strange at first to go through the ritual of bargaining, but in time, I developed the habit and used it to good effect. At that time in Singapore, there were night markets (known in Malay as Pasar Malam) in many districts throughout the city. The road was closed off, and stalls were set up selling a myriad of household goods, clothing, and even paintings. I soon got to know where and when these night markets would occur, and before long, the bare walls of my official residence were filled with paintings and fabrics and even local artefacts. One such purchase was a pair of wooden puppets known locally as Wayang Golek. Wayang Golek are wooden doll puppets that are operated by rods connected to the hands of the puppeteer whose deft hand movements made the puppet move as he used the puppet to bring to life the story that he was telling. These puppets came from the Indonesian Island of Java, where they were used to tell stories, and were, in effect, a form of theatre relating historical or religious events, including the Ramayana and the Mahabharata, which are ancient epics of Hinduism from India. (Prior to the arrival of Islam in Indonesia, the main religion was Hinduism with Buddhist overtones.)

Anyway, I arranged these puppets hanging on strings on a wall facing each other – one was male and the other female. Quite often, when I came downstairs in the morning, they were no longer facing each other but were back-to-back. Debra maintained that these puppets had fallen out during the night and no longer wished to face each other. I argued that it was simply something to do with the tension of the string or the movement of air in a large airy house with high ceilings. She, however, maintained that my Western background simply did not allow me to understand the mystic ways of the East.

It is a fact that even today, many societies in the East have overtones of mysticism and superstition that a Westerner finds hard to believe or accept. Certainly, soothsayers and Chinese geomancers enjoy a power that is difficult to understand, and I certainly found that in Indonesia, in particular, these experts in mystic ways play an important role in the everyday life of the populace. Folklore had it that when the Hyatt Hotel first opened on Scotts Road in Singapore, it was losing money. The owners were said to have consulted a geomancer who explained that as the main doors to the hotel faced straight out onto the street, the hotel's luck fell out of the doors every time they were opened. His advice was to set the doors at an angle of 20% to the street, thereby preventing the outpouring of luck, and when this was done, the hotel began to be successful. I cannot prove or disprove the story, but the main point is that whether it was true or not, people believed it.

In the course of my duties in Singapore, I got to know S R Nathan, who would go on to become the President of

Singapore. He was a great interlocutor, and we became close friends to the extent that he would regularly invite me for dinner at his home to enjoy his wife's fantastic curries.

Royal Visits to Singapore

The daily diplomatic grind was relieved when special events or VIP visits occurred, and during my time in Singapore, Royal visits and the like came along to inject some color into our lives. During my time in Singapore, Prince Charles and, later on, Princess Margaret made Royal visits to the Island Republic.

The visit by Prince Charles was my first royal visit and was preceded by a reconnaissance visit by his protection officer, Paul Officer, who, in effect, was Officer Officer! I invited Paul to join my then girlfriend Debra and me to dinner during his visit, and we became close friends. When Prince Charles arrived, it soon became clear that Paul had briefed the prince more than well as his first words when I met him off the plane were, "where is Debra!" He went on to ask if she was on the program and when I said no, he said that perhaps she should be on the program. As a result, Debra was put on the program and had to seek the permission of her British boss at work if she could take time off to accompany Prince Charles. She was unsure whether he really believed her or not! During the visit, Prince Charles visited the United World College and toured the campus, where he took time to chat with the students.

He stayed at the Istana, the official residence of the President of Singapore. On an evening free of engagements, he asked if I would like to join him for dinner on condition that I wear jeans and a casual shirt, and when I asked why jeans and a casual shirt, he said so that he could also wear jeans and a casual shirt. So, there we were in a posh dining room in the Istana, dining in jeans and casual shirt whilst being waited on by the Istana staff in all their finery. It was a most laid-back evening, and I must say he was a charming dinner companion free of airs and graces.

Escorting Prince Charles on visit to Singapore

Prince Charles and I at United World College in Singapore

I am firmly against using Royal tittle-tattle to brighten what might otherwise be a dull book, but a couple of snippets that occurred during the visit by Princess Margaret are not just tales out of school but serve to illustrate something of her make-up. During her visit, she wanted to make some purchases, and we found ourselves in one of Singapore's shopping malls. Whilst she was looking at some fabrics, the screw holding her spectacles to the frame came out and was lost. As any spectacle wearer can attest, this event threatened to spoil her afternoon, and she sought my assistance. I took her spectacles from her and visited a shop of B P De Silva on another floor, where a very obliging man repaired the spectacles in an instant, and when I told him who they belonged to, he refused to charge for the service. She was surprised when I returned the spectacles to her a few minutes later and laughed when I related that the man who had repaired them had pronounced them to be dirty and had cleaned them before returning them to me. She was even more surprised when I told her that the man refused to make any charge for his services and even more so when I told her that her knight in shining armor was none other than the father of Prime Minister Lee Kwan Yew. She insisted on thanking him personally, and he was quite delighted when she appeared in person to express her thanks.

At that time, Singapore Airlines ran a joint service with British Airways using Concorde, and at the end of her visit, she was due to fly back to the UK on Concorde. On the morning that she was due to leave, the High Commission received an anonymous call from a man with an Irish accent who claimed that there was a bomb on the Concorde flight that she was about to board. As this was at the height of the troubles with the IRA, the threat had to be taken seriously, and after a series of communications with the Royal household in London and Scotland Yard, it was decided that the aircraft should be quarantined, and I was obliged to attend a meeting with the Singapore Government Crisis Committee. Following this, all the baggage was removed from the aircraft, which was searched by counter-terrorist experts from the Singapore Government. In the event, nothing untoward was found, and both governments agreed that the flight could go ahead. This all took an inordinate amount of time, and the High Commissioner was obliged to entertain his guest for several extra hours and get his kitchen staff to provide an unscheduled lunch.

I should perhaps add at this point that the Singapore visit was the last leg of a tour of South East Asia, and prior to arriving in Singapore, she had picked up a stomach bug that caused her considerable discomfort and regular toilet visits. It says something about her that she never complained and got on with her Royal duties as best she could (although she did insist that I made sure where toilets were situated along our route). When she eventually arrived at the airport to board Concorde, as was my habit, I had avoided the VIP line and was standing under one of the vast wings of the aircraft, and after saying all the official farewells, she began to climb the steps to the aircraft. When she was about halfway up, she looked to her right and spotted me standing back under the aircraft wing. She came back down the steps through the VIP line-up and came over to me and said that she understood that I had had a very busy morning and expressed her thanks. An unnecessary gesture, perhaps, but one that speaks volumes of her character.

London Posting and Birth of My Darling Daughter Aurora

All too soon, my posting in Singapore came to an abrupt end and I was posted back to the UK. As I was due in London within a week Debra was left to pack up all our belongings and then set off for London to begin a new life in a new country.

We bought a small house in Herne Hill in South London, which was quite convenient as, in the summer, I could walk the three or four miles to work. Once she had the house running to her satisfaction, she really needed something else to fill her time as I was obliged to work long hours, and she got quite lonely. She found a job as secretary to the legal officer on the main board of EMI Music. It was an ideal choice as she found the work most interesting and exciting as a procession of world music stars came to her office with their agents to sign new contracts. The job also had its perks, as there was a free bar in the office, and on one occasion, when I picked her up from work, the Chairman and worldwide CEO, Bhaskar Menon, who was visiting the London Board Room announced when I entered the office, "Brian is here bring out the Dom Perignon." Other perks included free records and tickets to all pop and classical concerts in London. We enjoyed sitting in the Royal Box at Wembley Stadium watching the Rolling Stones concert in the company of Billy Connolly, and on one occasion at Wembley Arena, Diana Ross came down from the stage and held my hand as she sang her hit record "Reach Out and Touch."

We enjoyed a varied social life in Herne Hill until Debra became pregnant with our daughter Aurora. With Debra being a Singapore national, we decided that it would make sense for her to have our child in Singapore, where she had family support and an excellent general practitioner who we both knew well and trusted. By reason of being born there, Aurora could have access to Singaporean nationality, and should anything befall me, they could both return to Singapore and live there. Singapore does not allow dual nationality but the UK immigration law has a provision whereby the spouse and children of a British National, if Commonwealth citizens, can be granted a special visa called a Certificate of Entitlement, which in effect meant that they could both live and work in the UK and were even entitled to vote. So, Debra went home to Singapore to spend the final three months of her confinement in the comfort of her family home and under the care of our GP, Professor Lim Lean Huat. Although he taught medicine, he thoroughly enjoyed being a GP and, in his words, "it is wonderful to be able to treat three generations of a family."

In the last few days of her pregnancy, Debra was confined to hospital with pregnancy-induced hypertension, and I took some of the huge amount of leave that I was due to be with her for the birth. She was resting in hospital and was given oral tablets to induce labor which didn't work. After one day's rest, an intravenous drip was used to induce labor. When Aurora's arrival was imminent, Professor Lim was summoned by the hospital staff. As it happened at that very moment, a huge tropical storm erupted, and poor Professor Lim had to struggle through a traffic jam to get to the hospital in time. As he entered the labor ward, he shouted to Debra, "I need to scrub up, so don't push," and almost as soon as he reached her side Aurora emerged into the world. As soon as he announced that Aurora was healthy and had a full complement of fingers and toes, he said that my job of being present at the birth was done, and I should go off and give the good news to her parents whilst he saw to Debra and cleaned up Aurora.

I was pleased that I was able to be with Debra for the birth and especially pleased that she was delivered by Professor Lim, who is still our GP today and, indeed, is also Aurora's GP today in Singapore. (Debra herself was, in fact, delivered by Professor Benjamin Sheares, who later went on to become the President of Singapore!) Aurora spent the first two weeks of her life in Singapore, after which we flew back to the UK. We were blessed with a child who was a most contented baby, and before long sleepless nights were a thing of the past, and we enjoyed watching her development.

We enjoyed a varied social life in Herne Hill and made many friends that we are still in touch with today. The local beat officer from the Metropolitan Police was a regular visitor; our home becoming one of his "cup of tea spots", and the local Catholic priest Father Peter Clements was a regular guest when we had parties. Peter Clements was a wonderful priest, and when Aurora was at the crawling stage, she took to crawling around the church during the service. When Debra rushed to recover her, he himself picked her up and held her in his arms whilst giving the sermon. He was a man of great intelligence and wit, and whilst he didn't suffer fools gladly, he looked after his congregation with a high degree of pastoral care. As it happened, most of the Parish Council were like me, Protestants who were married to Catholics and on one occasion, he said in his sermon that when a man arrived at the gates of heaven, St Peter announced it was a quiet day, and he gave him a guided tour. At the end of the tour, he asked if the man had any questions and the man said that he was unsure why at the bottom corner, there were a lot of people with paper bags over their heads. St Peter laughed and said that they were the Catholics and that they liked to think that they were the only ones there!

On another occasion when I was chatting to him over coffee after the church service, I remarked that I had noticed several Catholic brothers in his church but no nuns. He threw his head back with great laughter remarked "Nuns – the KGB in drag!"

Herne Hill was a great location as we had Brixton Market close at hand, and Dulwich Park was only a short distance away. We spent many happy summer days in the park with Aurora, and she took her first steps there. We had a super local pub only 400 yards away run by an excellent landlord who kept a Rolls Royce motor car in his garage. He was a tenant as opposed to a manager, and the Brewery inspectors were only allowed over his threshold with a prior appointment. He kept an African Grey parrot in a cage on the bar, and this parrot would drink tea from a cup. It had a vast repertoire of sayings and was even able to imitate the clink of empty bottles being tossed into the plastic container under the bar. He had made his money running a very successful oyster bar and pub in South London, and his Herne Hill pub was for him, a semi-retirement spot where he could drink with friends and acquaintances. For us, it was a wonderful oasis where we made many friends and spent many happy evenings.

In time the Herne Hill house became a bit small for the three of us, and we bought a much larger new house in Bromley, which was built on a hill and from our lounge and bedroom, we enjoyed wonderful views over South London and were on the flight path of Concorde aircraft on their way into Heathrow. It was quite a sight to see Concorde flying relatively low as it made its approach. Whenever we heard the distinctive sound of the aircraft, we would run to our balcony and watch as it almost majestically made its way into the airport. In the summer months, we had a barbeque on the balcony on most evenings and on winter nights, we often enjoyed vintage port with Stilton Cheese and digestive biscuits.

Overseas Posting to Tanzania

After five great years running a department based in London, I was due to be posted to Tanzania in East Africa, and we had to look for tenants for our house and to prepare for the posting. Part of this preparation was studying the Kiswahili language, which has diabolical grammar. Preparation was the operative word as Tanzania at that time was in a poor state economically, largely due to President Nyerere's policy of African socialism. There were supermarkets that were obliged to open for business every day in order to keep their license, but the shelves were more or less empty save for a few tins of local coffee and handicrafts. We were, however, able to have four orders of dry goods a year and two shipments of frozen food shipped out from the UK. We ordered from a catalogue, but that took time, and the shipping time to Dar es Salaam took some weeks. Can you imagine having to work out how many frozen turkeys you would need for Christmas diplomatic entertainment when you made the order in June?

As we were due to arrive between shipments, the Foreign Office advised us to include a sizeable amount of dry goods in our heavy baggage. As Dar es Salaam didn't have much in the way of entertainment, we included a boat in our heavy baggage so that we might enjoy the pleasures of the Dar es Salaam Yacht Club social life and spend our free time sailing to offshore islands. When the shippers did an audit of our goods, they announced that we had spare capacity in terms of volume so we decided to fill that space with toilet rolls. We went off to our supermarket and arrived at the checkout with four trolleys filled with toilet rolls, and the checkout lady said to Debra, "have you got a problem, dear?!"

The road network in Tanzania at that time was basic, to say the least, and even in the town of Dar es Salaam there seemed to be more potholes than tarmac. Out of town, the roads were just dirt tracks, and we took the Foreign Office advice to take with us a four-wheel drive vehicle. We ordered a Range Rover and were invited to go to Solihull to the Range Rover test track to be taught by their experts how to get the best out of a four-wheel drive vehicle in the bush. That was a wonderful offer by Range Rover, who were sensibly keen for British Diplomats to be driving a premium British vehicle on a posting, thereby becoming an efficient way of advertising their vehicles. Our instructor was a skilled veteran, and he really put Debra and me through our paces. We drove up and down dirt hills with a 45% slope and learned to drive through deep water without killing the engine. I thoroughly recommend this driving course for anyone not used to driving four-wheel drive vehicles. This knowledge saved Debra from driving into a deep hole hidden in a puddle in Dar es Salaam. It is worth pointing out that Land Rover were extremely helpful and recommended that we not specify power windows in our Range Rover due to the likely problems if they should go wrong in a third-world country and so we had hand-operated windows.

We eventually got to Tanzania and waited with pregnant anticipation for our baggage to arrive, including our boat and Range Rover. Until the arrival of heavy baggage, you had to manage with basic belongings shipped out by air freight. The wait for the food in our heavy baggage would have been a serious problem, but the wife of the Head of the British Council in Tanzania came to our aid by raiding their own stock.

A Greek sisal millionaire had built our Dar es Salaam house, and it was certainly a grand dwelling with large rooms and high ceilings. The kitchen was particularly impressive, with ample space for our six chest freezers which were essential, given the amount of entertaining we were obliged to do as part of our representative duties. The house was situated next to the house of the President of Tanzania, which had numerous peacocks in the garden. Mrs. Ghandi had gifted a pair of peacocks to the government of Tanzania, and after a few years, they had bred to the extent that they outgrew the government house next to us and migrated to our property. Whilst it was nice to see these magnificent birds strutting around the garden, they could be very noisy, especially when they fell off their perches in the trees at night, letting out startled cries. They could be quite territorial, and one male bird in particular, used to attack his reflection in our patio doors, leaving ugly scratches on the glass.

Our garden was huge, and in addition to mature trees, we had spacious lawns and a useful vegetable garden. We also had stables and a paddock on the grounds left over by our predecessor. Crime was a serious problem as the economic situation in the country drew poor people into a life of crime and the number of illegal weapons in the country (a product from the Ugandan war) meant that armed robberies were a real problem that we had to guard against. Heavily armed gangs carried out break-ins coming in through the roof in many cases. As a result, our home had steel bars in the roof space to prevent access, and we literally slept in a jail with the route to our bedrooms fitted with heavy steel grills complete with stout padlocks. The telephone system was less than perfect, and we had radios in our public rooms and bedrooms which we could use to summon assistance. We were provided with security guards, one of whom was armed with a bow with poisoned arrows, and he maintained that he shot a burglar dead some years earlier. Our property was surrounded by high fences topped with razor wire, and we had airlock gates preventing would-be intruders from following us into the property when we came home.

We inherited some domestic staff from our predecessor but also hired additional staff, including two nannies, to look after Aurora, who was two years old when we arrived. The nannies each worked two full days and then had two days off. These two girls were most willing to learn, but they had come straight from their villages and needed constant supervision and training. To run such a huge house and entertain, we needed a full complement of staff; fortunately, some of them knew the house well. Not long after we arrived, Debra decided that our garden boy Elikana should be promoted to become an indoor steward. I must admit that

I was unsure whether he would cope, but he was a quick learner and willing to adapt. At that time in Tanzania, beverage bottles did not have labels, and one could only identify the contents by reference to the color of the crown cap. In the beginning, Elikana got his colors mixed up, and guests were treated to gin and soda and whisky with tonic. Actually, both were quite pleasant drinks, and maybe we should have patented the idea.

Eventually, our heavy baggage arrived, and we were able to enjoy the freedom of having our own Range Rover with a second car, a Peugeot 504, which was an ideal African car. There were no street maps, GPS or street signs, and we had to find our way around by trial and error, and getting lost was part of the fun. The infrastructure was basic, and when you stayed in a hotel, you had to be sure to bring along your own light bulbs and toilet paper, as they were usually missing. There were very few restaurants that one would be happy to eat at, and most expatriates and wealthy Africans entertained at home or joined a club. There were two clubs used by expatriates. The Gymkhana Club had a golf course of sorts, although there were no greens, and you were obliged to putt out on a mixture of oil and sand that was rolled into something resembling a flat surface. We weren't really into golf, so we joined the Dar es Salaam Yacht club, where we managed to arrange a good mooring for our boat.

The Yacht Club was an oasis of calm away from the hubbub of the streets of Dar es Salaam complete with beggars, some of whom had leprosy – I should add that their disease did not prevent us from assisting them with donations. The yacht club had good food and an excellent bar, and we spent most weekends sailing during the day, followed by sundowners and a good meal in the evening. During the week, Debra and Aurora spent many happy hours wallowing in the pools on the beach and both became quite tanned. In one memorable evening, the Yacht Club laid on a film evening, and we watched the movie, which was projected onto a screen that was a sheet hanging from a frame and moved in the breeze. The film, appropriately enough, was Out of Africa, which was filmed in neighboring Kenya and was most appreciated by the old African hands, some of whom, we were led to believe, had bit parts in the film as extras.

There were many uninhabited islands a few miles off the coast, and on weekends, we picnicked on the silver sand beaches. A favorite pastime was to put on a mask and snorkel and hang on to the back of the boat whilst it drifted across reefs with a fantastic variety of marine life. Our boat had a fast hull designed to plane with a big outboard engine and had a small cabin which was used by Aurora and her friends to play house. The Yacht Club had a wide variety of boats ranging from ocean-going yachts and motor-powered vessels to dinghies and the like. There were quite a few Hobie Cats, the owners of which organized a regular series of races. As they were inclined to push the envelope, especially in gusting conditions, there were many capsizes, and motorboat owners like me were always in great demand as safety vessels during the races. It was all entirely voluntary, but I must admit to receiving several cold beers in the club bar in the evenings as thanks.

Dar es Salaam Yacht Club Bar and Restaurant

View from the bar

The national language of Tanzania (formerly Tanganyika) is Swahili, more properly known as Kiswahili, and about six months prior to our posting, Debra and I were required to attend language tuition. The language is based on an East African Bantu language and has Arabic grammar bolted on. Nouns are divided into nine classes singular and nine classes plural, and the whole sentence follows the noun class. For example, there are many different words for "good" depending on which class of noun is used, and whether the word is singular or plural. A good child is mtoto mzuri, and good children watoto wazuri, with zuri being the root word for good. A good knife is kitu kizuri, and good knives are vitu vizuri. All very confusing, and I am pleased to report that not all Tanzanians got the noun classes right all the time. This is partly due to the fact that Kiswahili was originally the language of the coast, and the inhabitants in other areas had their own language or dialect. For example, one of our maids came from the warrior Wahehe tribe who spoke Kihehe, which was quite different and distinct from Kiswahili, and Aurora grew up speaking both Kiswahili and Kihehe, as well as English. Whilst senior government officials invariably spoke good English, household staff and market traders only spoke Kiswahili and their home dialects. It was important, therefore, to learn to speak the language at a reasonable level, especially if you wanted to haggle over prices in local markets.

Needless to say, there are not too many British nationals who speak Kiswahili. This allowed me to create a special experience for a Kiswahili speaker many years later. Debra and I were on holiday in Scotland and visited Holyrood Palace in Edinburgh. We noticed a tourist who was enjoying taking photos of the palace, and I remarked to Debra that he looked like a typical East African. I went over to him and greeted him in Kiswahili, and asked him how he was. He was so shocked, but when he recovered, so pleased, and this incident would no doubt be repeated in his tales of his Scottish holiday. In fact, he came from Kenya, which also has Kiswahili as its national language.

Whilst the supermarkets had little or no goods to sell, it was possible to purchase the basic staples such as fruit, vegetables, and eggs in local markets. These so-called markets were little more than makeshift structures at the side of a road, and one had to push and shove one's way through the hordes of local shoppers. All this in oppressive tropical heat, more or less acceptable on a dry day, but much less welcome during the rainy season when you were obliged to trudge through mud. Beef could be purchased, but we were advised by the FCO medical team to avoid local beef, as it was infected. Similarly, milk cows were infected with TB, so fresh milk was out of the question. Good quality pork and bacon products were available, but only on a restricted basis if you had the appropriate connections, and usually, you had to buy a whole pig. Fortunately, we had a large butcher's table in the kitchen and Debra and a friend of hers became skilled butchers. The Syrian Ambassador was a neighbor, and whilst he enjoyed hunting, he did not enjoy eating game meat. When he came back from the hunt, his driver would appear at our gate with a carcass over his shoulders, which our staff soon butchered and put in the freezer. We used this meat to entertain contacts in the African National Congress (ANC), who enjoyed game meat and were always ready to accept our invitation to dinner.

There were many ANC refugees in Tanzania and the ANC School was situated there. One of the ANC officials named Delukufa had a super sense of humor and would always tease Debra that someday he would marry Aurora, who at that time, was about three or four years of age. Many years later, I was at a cocktail party in the garden of the residence of the British Ambassador in Jakarta, when across the garden, I spotted a man who looked like my old friend Delukufa. He saw me looking at him, and his face began to show some concern, but eventually, the sides of his mouth turned up into a grin, and he came across and greeted me in Kiswahili. When I greeted him back in Kiswahili as Delukufa, he informed me that Delukufa had been a nom de guerre and that his real name was Sidney Kubeka, and he was now the South African Ambassador to Indonesia. He was still a bachelor, and a few weeks later, in connection with South African National Day, he invited Debra and me as his guests to a reception at his official residence for South African Nationals. I was unable to attend as I was out of Jakarta, but Debra went along, and he made a speech jokingly introducing her as his future mother-in-law, then went on to publicly thank her and me for our hospitality to him and his colleagues in Tanzania. A nice gesture! It should be noted that every one of the South African guests came up to Debra to congratulate her!

He had arranged for me to visit the ANC School in the west of Tanzania, and when I teased him that they were using Marxist Leninist literature in the school, he challenged me to do something about it. I duly took up the challenge, and in time, the British government supplied free of charge good quality textbooks in the English language to the school as part of an aid program.

Prime Minster Julius Nyerere retired in 1985 and was replaced by Vice President Ndugu al Haj Ali Hassan Mwinyi, who was our next-door neighbor. On taking power, Mwinyi set about taking steps to reverse the African Socialist policies of Nyerere by relaxing import restrictions and encouraging private business. He was a Muslim, but very much a moderate, and when Muslim fanatics attacked pork butcheries, he put a stop to their activities and made clear that individual freedom of religion was a keystone of Tanzanian culture. His attempts to kick start the economy were successful, and before long, small roadside shops, known in Kiswahili as Dukas, sprung up on the roadside manned by smiling Tanzanians. It is my view that Nyerere's attempts at introducing his Doctrine of African Socialism were doomed to failure as Africans, or at least Tanzanians, were capitalists at heart.

One day Debra noticed one of our maids scolding some children who were climbing a tree by our front gate. She asked the maid whose children they were and was told that they were, in fact, the children of the President. Debra made clear that they were welcome to come into the compound and play with Aurora. Later in the day, Debra went into the kitchen and found Aurora playing on the floor with one of the President's children, Halima, who was a little older than

Aurora, who at that time was four years. Debra noticed that whilst Aurora was drinking from a glass, Halima was drinking from an old yoghurt cup. Debra queried this and was told by the maid that Halima could not be trusted with a glass! Needless to say, that was soon put right! The wife of the President had seen Debra taking photos of the peacocks with a fancy camera, and our maid said that the President's wife had asked if we could take some photos of her daughter. This was agreed, and her daughter came round a few days later in a nice dress, ready to be photographed. Debra duly photographed her, and I sent the negatives off to London, where we had them enlarged and framed in nice frames. That gesture was much appreciated and is an example of basic but effective diplomacy.

There is a saying which reckons that on safari in Kenya, you will find a minibus with 12 people looking at three lions, whilst in Tanzania, you will find two people in a Land Rover looking at a pride of 24 lions. There was a lot of truth in that story, and the range and quantity of game in Tanzania were excellent. There are many conservation areas in the country, and one of the most famous is the Ngorongoro Crater, which is the largest inactive and unfilled volcanic caldera in the world. The crater is 2,000 feet deep, and the floor area is 100 square miles and filled with 25,000 animals. The drive down the 2,000 foot cliff was most exciting as the track was simply carved into the side of the wall of the caldera, and a few inches from your tire was a steep drop. You had to be accompanied by an official guide, and his knowledge was excellent, and we were amazed at the number of white and black rhinos in the relative safety of the crater.

We certainly enjoyed our safari trips to the many game parks, and on one occasion, we were one of five families in four-wheel drive vehicles on safari in the north of the country. Maps were non-existent, and we navigated our way by route instructions. Inevitably we got lost and pulled into a Masai village to seek assistance. The men all got out of the vehicles to meet with the elders and the women and children remained in the vehicles. When we were gone, Debra became aware of someone by the passenger side of the vehicle, and when she looked up, there was a Masai warrior complete with loincloth, spear, and shield, and hair covered with ochre. She wound down the window and greeted him in her best Kiswahili. "Hujambo Bwana, Habari gani." He replied in perfect English, "Good afternoon, Madam. Are you lost?" It turned out that he had just finished a degree at Oxford and had returned to the Serengeti to kill a lion to prove his manhood before going back to study for a PhD. This was a perfect example of dislocation of expectation that we came to experience in Africa. It should be noted that the Masai no longer kill lions to prove their manhood and now join in efforts to protect lions from poachers!

Debra with a group of Masai women

On another occasion, we were driving alone on a safari trip and in the afternoon pulled into a village to purchase a cold soft drink at a roadside stall. As was normally the case, we were soon surrounded by locals who were keen to chat. One of them asked if it was water or petrol that was dripping under our Range Rover. On inspection we found that it was petrol and they directed us to a roadside car mechanic workshop where the owner directed us to drive our vehicle over a rough hole by the side of the road. His team of mechanics got into the hole under the vehicle and soon removed the sump guard from our vehicle and identified that a stone had become lodged between the sump guard and the fuel tank and had punctured the tank. His team removed the tank and he said that he would repair it by brazing the hole in the tank. The tank was drained and prepared for brazing. When he saw the look of concern on my face, he said that if we were in the west, he would fill the tank with an inert gas, but as we were in Africa, he would rinse the tank with diesel, and then rinse three times with soapy water, then three times with clean water, then drop a lighted match into the tank to burn off any petrol fumes that might be left. This he did and he soon had the tank brazed. As it was getting late and I didn't want to drive for too long in the dark with wild elephants and the like roaming around, I tried to hurry him along and asked if he could get the tank put back on the vehicle. He grinned in the way that only East Africans can and said that the job was not yet complete. He went off and came back with a block of tar which he melted with a blow torch, allowing the molten tar to flow onto the brazed area thus ensuring that it would not rust! The job was soon completed and he handed me the bill which was certainly a fair price for the work done. When I offered him some additional money as a tip for his workmen, he again grinned and said that he had already included the tip in the bill price. I did, however, take a few of his business cards and promised to push them around friends with a recommendation.

I must say that we were more than happy with our Range Rover and with the Land Rover company. Land Rover had a small operation in Tanzania, and they worked in conjunction with the British Government in a Land Rover recovery drive which was part of a British aid program. I should point out that a Land Rover is a very sturdy vehicle in that it is built on a strong metal chassis, and all the body panels are manufactured from rust-free aluminum. There were literally hundreds of land rovers in the country and many of them were very old. The UK Government/Land Rover scheme was to strip down to the basic chassis all such Land Rovers and rebuild them using serviceable existing parts together with brand new replacement parts as required with the result that these old, rugged machines were given a new life essentially as new vehicles as part of the UK aid scheme.

At that time, there was a law in Tanzania that you were forbidden to photograph any government structure for security reasons. One day we were driving along a road when we encountered a Masai with a huge herd of cattle. Debra got her camera out and was about to photograph him and his cattle when I noticed that there was a bridge in the shot. I yelled for her to stop, and she did so just in time, as at that moment military men in uniform surrounded our car and at gun point, they instructed me to get out of the vehicle and hand over my camera as they said that we had photographed a bridge. I refused to get out of the vehicle, but did produce my diplomatic ID and pointed out the diplomatic plates on my vehicle. Nevertheless, they reached in and seized the camera through the driver's window. Again, I pointed out that I was a diplomat and said that I was prepared to let them have the film from the camera, but I demanded that they return my camera in order to prevent a diplomatic incident which would get them in serious trouble - it is in times like this that a good command of the language is essential. I managed to get the camera back into my hands and opened the back, and handed the roll of 35mm film to the officer. He pulled the film all the way out of the cassette, examined it and said that I was right, I had not taken any photographs. Praying that Debra wouldn't laugh, I bade him goodbye, put the car in gear and drove off.

On another safari trip, a group of us expats in vehicles were heading for a "resort" where we could stay in rooms that were carved out of a solid cliff face. The last obstacle we encountered before we arrived at the location was a wide fast flowing river. There was no bridge and no ferry, but there was a sort of ferry consisting of planks lashed to several oil drums. The idea was that you drove your vehicle onto the platform of planks, and several strong men would pull the raft across the river using a thick wire that stretched from one bank to the other. The raft only took one vehicle at a time and clearly, I was going to be the last to get across. As it was getting dark, I suggested that Debra, Aurora, and the maid cross in one of the other vehicles and I would follow on and meet up with them at the "safari lodge." They all went off, and when my turn came, it was getting quite dark, and by the time we reached the other side, it was completely dark. I had to drive about two miles along a narrow cutting, through the jungle in total darkness, and out of the jungle came a huge bull elephant trumpeting with ears flapping as though it was about to charge. I stopped in my tracks, and we looked at each other for some time with him flapping his ears menacingly, but thank God he eventually lumbered off into the night.

I got to the lodge to join Debra and Aurora and was about to relate the tale of my encounter with the bull elephant when they had their own tale. It appeared that on the roof of our "room," carved into the rock, were several lizards over a foot long that were so clumsy that they kept falling off the roof on their heads. They were in panic mode, but fortunately, the maid and one of the lodge staff used branches from nearby trees to shoo most of them out of the room. Nevertheless, it was a good feeling to be sleeping under mosquito nets on that occasion.

East Africans were wonderful people with an acute sense of humor, even though most had little to be happy about. Health was a big problem, and prior to leaving the UK, we were obliged to have a series of injections for multiple illnesses. Cerebral malaria was a real problem, and I lost two excellent colleagues to this dreadful disease in Africa. We were obliged to take a cocktail of anti-malarial prophylactics for the time we were there, and they were so strong that you never felt completely well. Incidentally, one of the drugs was Chloroquine, later made famous by President Trump as a cure for Covid! The High Commission had a stock of various medicines and Novocain for dental visits, complete with syringes that were guaranteed to be unused. The local hospitals and doctors' clinics were of a mixed variety, and for anything remotely serious, we were shipped out to Nairobi or to London.

Our houseboy Elikana was married, and his wife gave birth to twins who later became sick. They had all the signs of malaria, and he took them to a local clinic which simply gave him some over-the-counter medicine. When he related the story, we intervened and took him, his wife and the twin babies to a reputable clinic, which after a blood test, easily diagnosed that they did indeed have malaria. We organized the provision of the right drugs, and I am happy to say that they both recovered from the dreadful disease.

Malaria was a scourge of East Africa, and many young children died, usually from dehydration, as the disease ravaged their bodies. We assisted the local Rotary Club, who prepared information leaflets in Kiswahili on the dangers and made small plastic spoons, the ends of which were the right size for salt and sugar to be given in a glass of clean water. Hopefully, we managed to save several lives with this simple yet effective campaign, but in all honesty, it was probably just a drop in the ocean.

Two common medical problems could arise even in home environments. One was a burrowing flea called a jigger which lived in the grass and bored into bare feet when you walked on the grass. Once they invaded the body, they would thrive and move around the body, often crawling out through the skin on an arm or a leg and should they take a route via the eye, it could cause blindness. Our house in Dar es Salaam had a large garden with lots of lawns and our household staff were instructed to ensure that Aurora was never allowed to walk barefoot on grass. Such were our efforts to prevent her becoming infected with jiggers that, to this day, she is uncomfortable walking barefoot on grass. The other dangerous parasite was the putsi fly which laid its eggs on washing hanging out to dry. Once the unsuspecting wearer donned the egg-infected clothes, the heat of his body hatched the eggs, and the hatchling would burrow itself in the skin and feed off the host. Usually, the existence of this parasite only became known when it tried to emerge from under the skin as a maggot. Local knowledge decreed that household staff should be instructed to iron clothes well with a hot iron, thereby killing off the eggs before they had a chance to hatch.

East Africa could always come up with the unexpected, both serious and humorous. The garden boy who replaced Elikana was a most willing young man but didn't always grasp the point. When I noticed that some of the flowers in the garden began to look quite dry, I instructed him that at 5 p.m. each day, he MUST water all the plants in the garden after the heat had gone out of the sun and before it went down. A few days later, I came home in a cyclonic thunderstorm only to see him watering the flowers whilst sheltering under an umbrella! His name was Doto, and from his name, we knew that he was a twin and was the second twin to come into the world. In East Africa, twins are either called Kulwa (the first born) or Doto (the second born). It seems that there are tribal superstitions regarding twins, and when they are born, they do not give them real names for fear that one or both will die and simply call them Kulwa and Doto!

We learned in our pre-posting briefing that Tanzania did not have and indeed had never had any television stations, and there were no televisions in the country. We decided nevertheless to bring our TV with us with a video cassette player so Aurora could be entertained by watching cartoons on the TV. The first time we set the TV up, our maids were excited and filled with anticipation and sat on the floor with Aurora whilst I put on the cartoon version of Jungle Book. The maids sat open-mouthed watching the DVD, and when it finished, I asked them if they had enjoyed it. One of them shook us with her reply in Kiswahili which was, "How did they teach the snake to speak?" I considered explaining the science of cathode ray tubes but decided to simply say that they were very clever.

East Africans, including Tanzanians, were wonderful people who, in spite of poverty, were always ready to smile. They had an acute sense of humor and were extremely sociable, happy to chat with foreigners (Mzungu in Kiswahili). One of my closest Tanzanian friends clearly had an interesting background and his family were certainly wealthy. Indeed, they were one of many families who suffered under Nyerere's African socialism policy, and their family home was seized as they were considered to be far too wealthy. On one occasion, we had arranged to go out to dinner with him and another Tanzanian friend of his called Chris. Perhaps I should explain that Tanzanians were well known for their attitude to dress sense. We were waiting in a bar for Chris to join us, and when Chris arrived, he appeared wearing a white suit, a black shirt, a white tie and white shoes. My friend burst out laughing and remarked that Chris looked like a "bloody negative"! He certainly had the ability to laugh at himself and his friends despite his family's historical problems.

The streets of Dar es Salaam were always crowded and the pavements were taken over by hawkers and beggars. Some of these beggars were suffering from leprosy and sat by the roadside, fingers and toes missing, with a beggar's cup by their side. Life was indeed tough, and quite often, the area of the holes in their clothes was greater than the area of the fabric. I remarked on this to a Tanzanian friend, as he remarked that whilst there was poverty in Tanzania, life was harder in other countries, and he maintained that he knew of a family in Mozambique who were so poor that they only had one gunny sack for use between them to wear, and had to take turns at going out. One effect of the poverty was that you became responsible for your household staff and their families, and Debra made regular trips to the Government grain store to buy maize for our staff (maize is a staple part of their diet). It was a haphazard system, and you were obliged to carry lots of money to pay off officials at various levels to buy a sack of maize. This was in the time of Nyerere when the country was essentially bankrupt, and these corrupt practices were made even worse when the maize arrived in sacks with "A gift from the United States of America" stamped on the sacks.

We were protected from food shortages by our shipments of dry goods and frozen goods, and the arrival of the containers was the cause of great excitement. This was especially so when the frozen food container arrived, and all Embassy staff members descended on the location with their household staff with cold boxes to ferry the frozen food home to be placed in the many chest freezers that were essential items in our kitchens. Time was of the essence, and after several trips, our freezers were stocked with turkeys and hams for Christmas and other goods that had to last us for six months. Dry goods were kept in a spare bedroom fitted out with wooden shelving with the air conditioner on round the clock. I should add that the frozen and dry food and duty-free alcohol were not only for our own consumption but also for entertainment purposes.

As mentioned previously, we were advised by the Foreign Office medical people against eating local beef as the animals were infected with TB. Seafood was also in plentiful supply and was cheap. Lobsters were in abundance, and the most common starter at dinner parties was lobster tail. We identified our own lobster supplier, who dived for lobsters close to our beach house. We had a deal with him that every lobster that he supplied that was alive we would buy and freeze, and this could amount to tens of kilos. He would also supply fish, and I must say that barracuda cooked with a blend of chilli and spiced paste in tinfoil was a recipe that Debra made famous amongst our friends. It was also possible to buy huge tiger prawns, and I well remember taking a cold box full of tiger prawns to a meeting in Zimbabwe and returning with Zimbabwean beef in the box. I was popular on both ends of the journey.

Like many postings, Tanzania had its good and bad points, but the bad points were also a plus as they tended to draw the diplomatic community closer together. Tanzania was a case in point as we had a relatively small diplomatic community, and national day receptions were largely attended by the same people. So, you got to know your fellow diplomats and government officials in a way that would not be possible on a posting to a large capital such as Paris, Bonn, Washington and New York. The absence of suitable restaurants meant that most entertaining was done at home, and one's guests tended to be drawn from the same diplomatic group. (One irony was that in spite of its dearth of acceptable restaurants, Dar did have a Disney Ice Cream shop which sold super ice cream. Of course, it was not actually an official Disney outlet, but that did not stop Aurora and her friends from making it a regular spot to visit.)

Diplomatic postings in a small developing country led to the birth of great friendships that were long lasting. Facebook has made it easier to keep in touch with friends all around the world, and we remain in touch with many. One such case involved the Secretary to the Papal Nuncio (Vatican Ambassador) in Dar es Salaam, a wonderful Liverpudlian priest called Monsignor Paul Gallagher. Being fellow Brits, he and Debra and I got on well, and in spite of his church credentials, he had a wicked sense of humor. Paul invited us to lunch one day at the Nunciature and insisted that we bring Aurora along as the nuns could entertain her whilst we ate. It transpired that the nuns had kept her busy by letting her help feed their pet rabbits that they kept in the garden. When it was Aurora's birthday, she received a birthday card showing nuns with bunny-type ears drawn on top of their heads. The card read, "Happy birthday from Father Paul and the Nunny Bunnies." We have kept in touch with Paul over the years, and he invited us to be his personal guests when he was ordained as an Archbishop at the Vatican. By this time, Aurora was at university in the UK, so we met her there and flew to Rome to attend the event which was quite spectacular. We were allocated VIP seats and were surrounded by a host of Archbishops and Cardinals. The ordination was followed by a reception at the English College in Rome, which was so well attended that it took about 20 minutes for us to climb the beautiful wide circular staircase to the second floor where the event was being held. However, we were not bored in this queue as we were entertained by five Irish priests discussing the signs and symptoms of acute dehydration and whether the whisky which surely awaited them in the reception would be sufficient to rehydrate them. Needless to say, we kept in touch with Archbishop Paul, who is now the Vatican Foreign Minister and represented the Pope at the funeral of Queen Elizabeth.

Catching up with Archbishop Paul after his ordination

Princess Anne visited Tanzania to visit facilities provided for poor and orphaned children by one of her favorite charities, the Save the Children Fund. This was the first of four countries she would visit in East Africa in connection with this charity. This involved flying in and out of remote airfields in light aircraft, and at the end of the tour of the Save the Children facilities, we arrived in our light aircraft ahead of her light aircraft and we chatted on the ground with the Captain of the Queens Flight who was waiting to fly her back to the capital Dar es Salaam. We could see a huge storm approaching, and the Captain of the Queens Flight advised us not to wait but to take off immediately. We duly took off from this strip, and at the end of the runway, there was a sheer drop of about 2000 feet. We climbed away, but as we did so the storm hit and the visibility was such that we were obliged to fly beneath the clouds, which were already low and had to effectively navigate using a road map as the storm tossed us around without mercy. It was a real white-knuckle flight, and we were relieved when we finally saw some familiar buildings near Dar es Salaam and landed safely. As a postscript to this story, the Princess asked the High Commissioner to arrange a dinner at the residence on her last night, so that she could thank all the people who had worked to make the visit a success. I understand that she did the placement, and I found myself sitting on her right side at the table. She was a most charming and laid-back dinner companion with great stories, and it was hard to believe that she was a princess! The topics we discussed over dinner must, however, remain untold, but I still have many happy memories!

Debra and I at our initial meeting with Princess Anne

Our posting in Dar es Salaam was due to come to an end when we received a signal from London asking us to stay on for an extra couple of weeks to look after Prince Charles (whom we had looked after in Singapore ten years earlier), who was due to visit Tanzania. This we duly did, and when the then Prince got down from the aircraft, he was met by the High Commissioner, who brought him across to the receiving line. Amazingly, Prince Charles greeted Debra and me by name and then hunched down to say to Aurora, "I know your Mummy and you Daddy, but I don't know who you are!" Part of the safari visit included overflying the migration of over a million wildebeests in a light aircraft which was a most spectacular event. We didn't think much more about the safari with the prince until a few weeks after we had returned to the UK when the headmaster of the local primary school that Aurora attended asked us to participate in an important meeting. When we were seated in his office, he asked Aurora's class teacher to explain what the problem was, and she said that we should be aware that Aurora told lies and lived in a fantasy world. When we asked what was behind this statement, she said that the previous Wednesday she had asked the Class if they knew whose birthday it was that day, and only Aurora knew that it was the birthday of Prince Charles. The teacher went on to say that when she asked Aurora how she knew, she had said that she was a friend of his. You can imagine the look on the headmaster's face when we told him that she was indeed a friend of Prince Charles and that we had recently spent ten days together with the prince on safari in Africa. Yet another example of dislocation of expectation!

Back to London

The next three years were spent in the UK and we settled into the more mundane British life with occasional overseas visits and I got to know many hotels, and if the Government had allowed me to collect air miles, I would have made a fine accumulation. However, it was strictly prohibited to do so on journeys paid for by the British taxpayer. Government regulations can be a pain, and I well remember that in Tanzania, there were two lifestyles available, one using the official exchange rate and one using the black-market rate. The black-market rate brought in ten times the number of Tanzanian Shillings than the official rate. We were forbidden to use the black market, and on one occasion, when Aurora was invited to a friend's birthday party, we struggled to find a present that we could afford at the official exchange rate and her friend was given a hair accessory as a present.

One of the countries I visited in this three-year period was Sri Lanka which was in the grip of terror campaigns by the Liberation Tigers of Tamil Eelam (LTTE), who were seeking independence for the north and east of the country and the Janatha Vimukthi Peramuna (JVP) a Marxist-Leninist communist group that was trying to overthrow the government. Curfews were in place, and it was surreal to be one of only 18 guests staying at a five-star hotel in the middle of Colombo. At that time, the JVP were a more immediate threat than the LTTE, and it is estimated that many thousands died in the JVP-inspired insurgency of 1987 to 1990. By early 1990 the government had imprisoned or killed most of the politburo, and the crisis ended, but the LTTE was to wage a terror campaign against the government for another 19 years before its leader Velupillai Prabhakaran was killed and peace was restored.

Overseas Posting to Sri Lanka

Little did I know when visiting Sri Lanka in 1989 and 1990 that by the end of 1990, I would be there on another overseas posting. Unlike the High Commission in Dar es Salaam which was on the upper floors of a rundown high-rise building, the Colombo High Commission was a neat four-story building set on its own grounds by the sea. It was straight into work for me, and Debra was kept busy putting Aurora into an international school and looking for a suitable house. It took several months to find a suitable house, but the wait was worth it as we eventually found a house in the middle of town close to the High Commission that was perfect for our needs. There began the business of finding household staff, but in the months it took to find the house, Debra had a solid grip on the Sri Lankan way of doing things, and we hired a husband-and-wife team and a teenage girl for household duties. The wife was a good cook, her husband was a good gardener, and the young girl was able to look after Aurora. Therefore, we thought we had our full complement to run the house. However, not long after we moved into the house, there was a severe cyclone and 70,000 were made homeless in the floods that followed. One of those affected by the floods was our dhoby man (clothes washer) who had lost his home. As a result, he and his wife and children moved into one of our staff quarters. Shortly thereafter, another man came calling at the house looking for a job. He was a 70-year-old who had been working as a cook for the Deputy Chief of Mission at the US Embassy and had been compulsorily retired due to age. He produced his passbook (a sort of workbook), which showed him to be called Arumugam and that he had started work as a kitchen coolie at the age of 14. We took pity on him and hired him, and he also moved into our property which fortunately had sufficient staff quarters. He was a wonderful old man who baked the most delicious bread and made spice buns and Danish pastries every afternoon. The house smelt wonderful and our waistlines were in serious danger. He fitted in well and we took care not to overwork him. He took time off each afternoon "to go for a walk" but we later learned that he actually popped into a nearby bookmakers to put a small bet on the horses.

He was quite sprightly, and his only health problem was that he was beginning to develop cataracts. Immediately following the big floods, Hema Premadasa, the wife of the President, called Debra and asked if she could put on a charity fashion show to raise funds for those made homeless. (I should point out that in Sri Lanka it became known that Debra was a former Miss Singapore, and as a result, a well-known Sunday newspaper would be adorned with photos of Debra taken at Diplomatic events and describing the outfits she wore.) Debra, of course, agreed and set up a committee of diplomatic wives and friends to plan the event. Many hours were spent persuading businessmen to sponsor the event, and one committee meeting was held in our dining room, and when the nearly blind Arumugam had finished serving tea to the ladies, he opened the door to a cupboard and tried to walk in, thinking it was the door out of the dining room. The poor man was most embarrassed, and we decided immediately to have his cataracts operated on at our expense. He was delighted, and Debra was also delighted when her fashion show managed to raise a considerable sum of money for the rehousing fund run by the President's wife. Arumugam stayed with us until the end of our posting when Debra arranged for a Singaporean friend who was married to a Sri Lankan, and had an extremely large house to give him a job in perpetuity so that he would never be homeless.

Our home in Colombo

The terror campaign by the LTTE affected all our lives, and during the three years we were in Sri Lanka we lost an untold number of close friends who were assassinated by the LTTE. The Commander of the Sri Lankan Navy, Admiral Clancy Fernando, had promised to take Debra to see Trincomalee in a Navy helicopter one Thursday morning, but two days before they were due to leave, he was blown up by an LTTE suicide bomber outside the Taj Hotel in the centre of Colombo. The New Zealand Cricket team was on tour in Sri Lanka at the time and was staying at the Taj, and most of the team came out of the hotel to see the scene of carnage. If you are not used to dealing with death, especially bodies that have been blown up and have suffered shrapnel effects, it can turn the stomach. It certainly affected the New Zealand team, many of whom wanted to abandon their tour of Sri Lanka there and then. New Zealand did not have an embassy in Colombo, but their embassy in Singapore asked if we could attempt to persuade their team to continue with the tour. The Defense Attaché and I spoke with them and managed to persuade most of them that all Sri Lankans loved cricket, and even the LTTE were cricket mad, and the chances of the LTTE harming any cricketer were beyond belief. I am pleased to say that most of them stayed on, and the tour continued without incident, just as we had predicted.

Probably due to their British Colonial history, Sri Lankans have a great love of cricket and rugby, and most schools have several teams of both to represent them in these sports. I was co-opted onto the committee of the Colombo Hockey and Football Club, a famous hockey, cricket and rugby club situated in Cinnamon Gardens, and I spent many happy hours watching rugby on Friday, Saturday and Sunday evenings when the heat had gone out of the sun. Rugby in Sri Lanka was quite unique, and after each match, we would move on to a social gathering where the result of the game was discussed in depth, and large quantities of beer and whisky were consumed before we saw off the hottest curries imaginable. Sri Lankan curries are something else and can best be described as dynamite. Fortunately, I had spent enough time in the east to be able to manage these spicy delights, but you certainly need a strong constitution to cope with both the alcohol and curries.

My job in Sri Lanka involved a good degree of liaison with the police. As a result, I was regularly invited to social evenings that the Inspector General of police would host for his 20 deputy Inspector Generals. These socials were held at the police HQ grounds, and we sat at a long table filled with bottles of Johnny Walker Black Label, buckets of ice and soda. Serious drinking went on from 7 p.m. until about 11 p.m. when a typical spicy curry was served. These guys could drink!

Sri Lankans loved to eat late, and when we first arrived in Colombo, we were invited to a dinner party, and the invitation said it would start at 7 p.m. We duly arrived at 7.05 thinking that was politely late enough. When we rang the doorbell, the host opened the door in his shorts and T-shirt, and his wife appeared in her dressing gown complete with curlers in her hair. There was a most uncomfortable hour where they took turns between entertaining us and getting dressed before the other guests began to trickle in between 8 and 9. We soon learned that 7 p.m. on the invitation meant turn up after 9 pm!

Sri Lankans have a great capacity for enjoyment and Sri Lanka parties were great affairs with music, laughter, and dancing, huge quantities of alcohol and of course their famous curries. Whilst we had to attend many diplomatic functions, we also had a wide circle of Sri Lankan friends who were perfect hosts. Debra's efforts with her charity fashion show had gone down well with the result that she appeared weekly on the fashion and gossip pages of the newspapers and we both became well known. To be well known in Sri Lanka could be two-edged sword as it might well make you a target for the LTTE. I certainly felt extremely uncomfortable when waiting in my car at traffic lights when a motorcyclist with a full-face helmet would pull alongside me. The LTTE used motorcycle suicide bombers, and you never could be sure if it was just a man on his way home or an LTTE terrorist who pulled alongside. Terrorism affected all facets of life and a visit to a supermarket or a hotel involved having your car searched before entering the car park. Police roadblocks would appear without warning, and undergoing security checks became a way of life. Bombs went off in the capital of Colombo and in most other areas of the country, but we did try to live as normal a life as possible. Security was tight both at the High Commission and at the US Embassy situated next door to our High Commission. This was in the very early days of mobile phones in Sri Lanka, and we relied heavily on radios for emergency communications. We shared a radio network with the US Embassy, and a radio message from the US Ambassador one morning that he was trying to get to work through the floods on the back of a high lorry was met with some mirth, but also praise for his willingness to plough through the floods with little pomp and ceremony.

The celebration of May Day on 1 May 1993 was, as usual, a public holiday. President Premadasa was out amongst the people in his armored Range Rover to attend a May Day rally. As was his style, the President got out from the safety of his vehicle to get closer to the people and check the arrangements for the May Day parade. As he did so, he was approached by a man pushing a bicycle, and as the man reached him, he detonated a bomb that was hidden on his body. Premadasa died immediately and 14 others, including a senior police officer, also died in the blast. Ironically, Premadasa's driver remained in the vehicle, unhurt even though the vehicle was close to the explosion.

There was an immediate clampdown by security authorities following the assassination, as many feared some retaliatory action would be taken. The leader of the opposition Lalith Athulathmudali had been fatally shot whilst addressing an opposition rally only eight days before Premadasa was assassinated, and some were quick to accuse Premadasa of being behind his death. A police investigation concluded that Athulathmudali had been assassinated by a Tamil youth who was an LTTE cadre. However, Premadasa's successor, President Chandrika Bandaranaike Kumaratunga, appointed a presidential commission to investigate the Athulathmudali assassination, and its final report published in 1997 laid the blame at the door of the late President Premadasa and security force personnel who were close to him. Subsequently, some members of the security forces were arrested together with underworld figures and were charged with conspiracy and aiding and abetting the murder. During the prosecution, three of those charged were killed, adding further fuel to the conspiracy theories.

In spite of the terrorism, Sri Lanka was a great posting. The warmth of the people showed through, and we made many wonderful friends that we are still in touch with today. The diplomatic community was very laid back and held together well. I well remember at a National Day reception greeting the Italian Ambassador with the customary polite diplomatic greeting of "Your Excellency," and he replied with a laugh saying, "I have told you before and will not tell you again we are good friends and should be on first name terms, and if you call me Excellency again, I will punch your ear!" On another occasion, there was an election for the board of governors of the International School, and one of the candidates was the Canadian Ambassador who, when introducing himself, did not announce that he was the Ambassador but simply said that he worked at the Canadian Embassy. The Malaysian Ambassador and his wife were close friends and he and Debra would tease each other over the rivalry between Singapore and Malaysia. He was a skillful diplomat and had a down-to-earth touch. It was with some amusement that he related that when he was a student studying at University in Scotland, he spent his Christmas holidays working as a part-time postman in my hometown of Hawick! However, diplomatic friendships are by their very nature short, and he was cross-posted to South Africa as the Malaysian Ambassador there. Sadly, it was the last time we were to meet with his charming wife Sara, who was tragically killed in a motor traffic accident in South Africa.

Another great friend in Sri Lanka was the Indonesian Ambassador, a charming man with a wicked sense of humor and an excellent host. Debra and I seemed to gravitate to him at Cocktail parties, and he could be relied upon to liven up a dull evening. Sadly, he suddenly became ill and was diagnosed with Japanese Encephalitis and had to be flown home seriously ill. I was able to assist his Defense Attaché, Colonel Rus Rusbandrio, with the arrangements and Col Rus and his wife Shirley became our close friends, and years later he worked for me in my company in Jakarta.

Cross Posting to Indonesia

All too soon it was our turn to leave Sri Lanka as we were cross posted to Indonesia and after our heavy baggage was packed up, we moved back into the Ramada Hotel for the last few days of our posting. We left Sri Lanka on an overnight flight, arrived in Jakarta in Indonesia the following morning, and moved into the Mandarin Hotel, just across the road from the British Embassy. After breakfast, I went straight into the office and left Debra to get on with the task of finding a suitable school for Aurora and to begin house hunting. House hunting is the bane of a diplomat's life, and I believe Debra looked at no less than 200 houses before we identified one that was suitable and within the budget set by the Embassy. We looked at both the British International School and the Jakarta International School (JIS) and in the end opted for JIS largely because it was closer to town, but also because the headmaster Niall Nelson had formerly been the Headmaster of the Dar es Salaam International School and we knew him and his wife Kay well. It was a good choice as before long Aurora announced that JIS was the best school she had ever attended and said she would be happy to end her schooling days at that school. The location of the school affected our house hunting, and, in the end, we decided that it was more important for her to be close to the school than for me to be close to the office. It was a good choice as school started at 7.30 in the morning and with tons of homework, she had an extremely long day. The distance to the Embassy was not too big a concern for me as we were up early every morning to get Aurora off to school. I left home at 5.45 a.m., and as there was little traffic at that time of the morning in those days, before Jakarta began to outgrow its infrastructure, I could be in the office a little after 6 a.m. The office opened for business at 8 a.m. and those two hours with no telephone calls or other interruptions were a golden time for catching up with paperwork!

Even in 1993, traffic conditions in Jakarta were beginning to become a problem and were a stark contrast to the less developed Jakarta I had known on my first visit there in 1977 when I was invited to take part in the second Jakarta Highland Gathering, which was and still is the largest Highland Gathering in the Southern Hemisphere. A Scottish friend in the Embassy in Jakarta who was a leading light in the Jakarta St. Andrews Society asked whether I could hand carry the medals for the winners of various events down to Jakarta from Singapore. My arms were six feet long by the time I got them through customs, but at least I got them there safe and sound. That was not my only task, as I was also invited to be the drum major of the day for the massed pipe bands at the closing ceremony. In addition to caber tossing, hammer throwing, and tug of war, the gathering also held competitions for pipe band quintets which consisted of three pipers, a bass drummer and a side drummer. Bands came from as far as Australia and Hong Kong, and there was keen competition. Scots living in Jakarta came along in kilts, and the color of the occasion was enhanced by the Highland and Scottish Country Dancers.

A great day was had by all, especially the local Indonesians, who were amazed to see men in "skirts" throwing telegraph poles around like they were matchsticks. The beer tents did a great business, and playing pipes, dancing, and tossing cabers is thirsty business even if you were only a spectator. In the evening, the Chieftain of the St. Andrews Society, Bernie McReady, who had previously played in goal for Celtic, held a reception at his home. Unusual for Scots, we did have a few drams and the highlight of the evening was witnessing the Pipe Sergeant of the Gurkha Pipe band setting off into the night with his more than tipsy Pipe Major over his shoulder.

Prince Edward visited Indonesia in March 1994 to formally open the new British International School, which had moved from its location in the middle of the town in Permata Hijau to a new campus on a 13-hectare site in Bintaro, about one and a half hours away. On the day of the visit, we were in a VIP convoy escorted by the Indonesian National Police Service, which cut the travel time by half. During the visit, the prince worked hard, and in addition to opening and touring the campus, he spent a huge amount of time chatting with the students, which went down greatly.

It was, therefore, great to be back in Jakarta, and I duly joined the St. Andrews Society and was soon co-opted onto the Committee of the Highland Gathering, which had gone from strength to strength in the sixteen years in between. I met up again with Bernie, and Debra and I made many friends in the St. Andrews Society. The Society held three main events during the year, the Burns Supper, the St. Andrews Ball and the Highland Gathering. By this time, the gathering had expanded and now included a ceilidh night called Scotland in Concert, which took place in a local hotel ballroom the night before the Gathering. The sponsors of the Gathering flew in caber tossing and hammer throwing "heavies" and also flew in Scottish entertainers for Scotland in Concert. I must say that I am far from convinced that it is a good idea to have hard-drinking Scots attend a ceilidh on the night before the Gathering, and there were many sore heads as the gathering got under way each year. One of the many pipe bands attending the gathering was the Sikh Pipe Band from Kuala Lumpur. We soon became close friends with them, and in 2019 a quintet from that band played at Aurora's wedding in Malacca in Malaysia, and played the principal guests and the bride and groom into the reception.

On the cocktail circuit

In addition to my Embassy duties, I was co-opted onto the Board of the British Chamber of Commerce, which at that time had set up a scheme in conjunction with the Liverpool Football Club to encourage young children to take up sport, and Liverpool players Ian Rush and Phil Neal came out to Jakarta to run coaching classes for these poor youngsters. They both took their duties very seriously, and in order to assist, I let Ian Rush have Debra's car, driver, and our bodyguard at his disposal whenever he was in Jakarta.

Ian Rush, Debra and I together with the driver and bodyguard

With Phil Neal in Jakarta

In addition to my general duties as a member of the Board of the British Chamber of Commerce, I also ran a weekly discussion group targeted at small and medium enterprises. I was able to guide these companies on the threats facing their businesses and more importantly, what they could do to ensure their safety and security. This group soon got off the ground and was well attended every week and continued long after I had retired from the Embassy.

Indonesia which straddles the equator is a huge country and has the largest Muslim population in the world. It consists of close to 18,000 islands stretching from Aceh in the West to Papua in the East over a distance of more than 5,000 kilometers and has around 300 languages. The unifying National Language is Bahasa Indonesia which is similar to Malay, but many inhabitants still use their traditional languages at home. Jakarta is the capital and Greater Jakarta is home to around 30 million people, many of whom have travelled from the outer islands to make their fortune in the capital city. The Island of Java, which has just short of 1,000 inhabitants per square kilometer, is the most populated island in the world. Indonesia lies on the "Ring of Fire" and earthquakes and volcanic eruptions are a part of normal life. It has 150 active volcanoes and the Toba "super volcano" which occurred some 75,000 years ago was arguably the largest volcanic eruption ever and caused a global catastrophe. We soon got used to earthquakes of various strengths and one quake was so violent that the water in our swimming pool at home swirled around like a whirlpool, and half the pool water surged out into the garden. More on earthquakes a little later!

Once we settled into our new home, we began entertaining. In the early days, Aurora was put in charge of ensuring the guests signed the guest book before being sent off to bed whilst the grownups got on with their evening. In my final year at the Embassy, she played a bigger part in assisting with our entertaining and was a most useful addition to the team. British Diplomats have to decide whether to bring their children along with them on overseas postings or send them to boarding school. Much depends on the quality of schooling available, and we were fortunate in that we were able to put her in adequate schools in all our postings. There are arguments both ways, and some children do very well in boarding school and get a lot out of it, but on balance, we consider that we made the right decision. There is no doubt that exposure to different cultures in their early years can have a beneficial effect, and I firmly believe that Aurora got a lot out of this exposure which has stood her well in adult life. (In fact, one of the three Doctors who were bridesmaids at her wedding was a classmate from Primary School in Jakarta!)

The British Embassy, housed in an old building in the middle of town, had been attacked by a mob of Indonesian activists on 16 September 1963 during the Indonesian Malaysian Confrontation. Even after extensive rehabilitation, it was, in my view, hardly fit for purpose. It has, however, been replaced by a new building better suited to represent British interests in Indonesia. However, it is worthy of mention that as the building was being attacked, a member of the Embassy Defense Attaché staff, Major Rory Walker, marched up and down in front of the Embassy playing his bagpipes as a measure of defiance as the mob pulled down the Union flag and burnt the Ambassador's car. Two days later, the mob returned and set fire to the Embassy. The attack on the Embassy was in retaliation for the formation of Malaysia by the British Colonial Government, a move that was opposed by the Indonesian Government which saw it as a ploy to enhance British control in the area, thereby threatening Indonesian independence. A peace agreement was signed by the new Indonesian President Soeharto in 1966.

Right across the road from the Embassy was the Hotel Indonesia, which was opened in 1962 by President Sukarno and featured in the film "A year of living dangerously." The film was set at the time of the overthrow of President Sukarno and centered on a group of foreign journalists on the eve of an attempted coup. The film was banned in Indonesia until after the fall of President Soeharto in 1997. By 1993 the hotel was becoming quite run down but was still a favorite of many tourists who came to take in the atmosphere of the faded grandeur of the hotel as depicted in the film. The hotel closed in 2004 and after a five-year renovation was reopened under the management of the Kempinski Hotel Group.

On January 8, 1996, a group of four Cambridge postgraduate students, two Dutch nationals, one German, and 21 Indonesians were kidnapped by the Papuan separatist Organisasi Papua Merdeka (Free Papua Movement), known as the OPM were held hostage. I was on leave and out shopping when I received a pager message to go to the Embassy immediately for a meeting with the Ambassador. My leave was cancelled, and I was soon on my way to the Sukarno-Hatta Airport, booked on a 10-hour flight to West Papua which at that time was better known as Irian Jaya. Upon my arrival in the provincial capital of Jayapura, I met with Indonesian officials and representatives from the Dutch and German Embassies as we endeavored to shed some light on the background of the kidnapping and the current situation of the hostages. In due course, the Indonesian military and intelligence organizations set up a forward base in Wamena in the Baliem Valley to deal with the kidnapping. The Baliem Valley was unknown to the outside world until the 1930s when an Australian pilot flew over the area, and even in the 1990s, the area was underdeveloped, and communication and transportation were difficult, to say the least. The International Commission of the Red Cross (ICRC) volunteered to take the lead in conducting negotiations with the leader of the kidnappers, Kelly Kwalik, and we were able to use the good offices of the ICRC to maintain contact with the hostages, and act as a link between them and their families.

Eventually, another member of the British Embassy and I were able to obtain permission from the Indonesian Authorities to travel to Wamena to act as a link between the British families and the ICRC and the Indonesian team. Little did I know at that time that I would make the same journey to Wamena many times over the next three and a half months as negotiations were conducted with the OPM. The journey to and from Wamena from the Irian capital Jayapura was not for the faint-hearted. There was no regular passenger air service in operation, and one had to negotiate with one of the transport aircraft companies that flew between Jayapura and Wamena. These aircraft had no passenger seats, and a seat was bolted in at the rear of the aircraft for any passengers brave enough to fly. On the inward journey to Wamena, the load was usually cement, bricks, and other construction materials, together with 40-gallon drums of petrol and diesel. On the way out, the load was regularly empty 40-gallon drums, and live pigs trussed up. These aircraft were not pressured, and as they flew over the central highlands to reach the valley, they lurched perilously close to rugged ridges. The door to the cockpit was always left open, and one could see the pilots with their oxygen masks in place as they were left struggling to get breath due to the altitude. Going in was not too bad, but on the way out, as the aircraft reached altitude, the drop in pressure caused the empty oil drums to expand with a loud bang. The bang startled the pigs, which began squealing and defecating, filling the cabin with their stench. It was always a relief to get one's feet back on terra firma at the end of these flights.

The weeks of waiting as the negotiations continued were a time of tension, but we were able to meet and bond with many indigenous tribesmen, and provided them with some extra income as we purchased Stone Age axes, feather headdresses, prized boar's teeth, and bows and arrows from them. These tribesmen, who were essentially Melanesian, lived a Stone Age existence with the men wearing only penis gourds and the women grass skirts. Before the arrival of Christianity, they were headhunters and cannibals, and inter-tribal battles were frequent. They lived in traditional wooden huts with thatched roofs and survived by breeding pigs and tending gardens in the jungle where they grew sweet potatoes and vegetables. The men are skilled hunters and the women, who seem to do most of the work, raised their children and pigs. When you visit a Papuan village in the central highlands, you really take a step back in time. On one occasion, when I visited a village, the headman brought out from a hut the mummy of a famous tribal warrior still sitting in the chair in which he was preserved by means of smoking. Pigs are an important part of their livelihood, and the women will often suckle sickly pigs on their breasts.

By early May, there appeared to be a breakthrough and Kelly Kwalik announced that he would free the hostages. The church floor was swept and the floor covered in freshly cut grass, and pigs were killed in preparation for a traditional Papuan pig feast. Feelings were running high but were dashed when at the last minute, on 9 May, Kwalik changed his mind and took off into the jungle with the hostages. As a result, the Indonesian authorities decided to launch a military effort to free the hostages, and they set off in pursuit.

On 15 May the military team caught up with the hostage takers. After a firefight, 9 of the 11 remaining hostages were released (during the negotiating phase, the kidnappers had released some of the original 26 hostages), but two Indonesian hostages were killed by their captors. We were then kept busy in Jakarta debriefing the four British hostages before repatriating them safely back to the UK to join their families, and the Mapenduma hostage incident came to an end.

There is, however, a sad postscript to the Mapenduma affair, as in addition to the two Indonesian hostages killed by the OPM, several others lost their lives. In mid-April a member of the Indonesian military team ran amok and shot dead 16 people in an aircraft hangar in Papua. Eight of the dead were from the military and five others were civilians, including a pilot from New Zealand. In the second week of May, an Indonesian military helicopter escorting the ICRC helicopter crashed, killing all on board. No military personnel were killed by the OPM during the raid on the OPM hostage takers, but five members of the military died when their helicopter crashed during the military operation.

My mode of transportation

Mummified body of a famous head-hunter

Life Threatening Illness

Shortly after the hostage crisis, I took ill with stomach pains, and the Embassy doctor diagnosed appendicitis and had me shipped off to a hospital in Singapore. The Singapore doctors were also of the view that I had appendicitis and I was duly operated on. When I came around, the surgeon said that he had removed my appendix, but he was far from convinced that the appendix was the problem, and ordered me to remain in hospital for further tests. After a barrage of tests, including a colonoscopy carried out by Dr Teh Lip Bin, it was decided that I could be suffering from colon cancer, and a further operation was scheduled. On the day of the second operation, I was visited by an old friend who was a surgeon and was from the medical practice I had used when posted in Singapore in the late seventies. He tried to reassure me and said that for old time's sake he would assist the surgeon in the operation, free of charge!

When I came round from the second operation, the surgeon informed me that that he had removed a large part of my colon that was being blocked by a sizeable tumor. The tumor was being sent off for a biopsy, but the odds were that it was cancerous. The biopsy confirmed that it was cancer and I was then put into the care of a renowned oncologist, Dr Tan Yew Oo, who had also attended to Lee Hsien Loong, who suffered from Lymphoma and went on to become the Singapore Prime Minister. He declared that as my cancer was considered to be Stage 3, I would need a year of chemotherapy and that my chances of surviving more than five years were slim.

In the meantime, I had to recuperate from the operation and, in spite of large doses of intravenous painkillers, I was in considerable pain. I had been fitted with a stoma which is a tube that runs from the colon to a bag that collects waste matter. As an accident of history, my niece from Scotland was nursing at that very hospital and popped in to see me from time to time. Debra slept with me in my hospital room, and my secretary from the Embassy in Jakarta, paid me a visit with greetings from Embassy colleagues. Colleagues from the US Embassy in Jakarta also visited and provided me with some reading matter to pass the time away. After a few days, I was put into the hands of a therapist who insisted I get out of bed and try to walk. Easier said than done! I not so silently cursed the poor fellow for putting me through the pain. However, he managed to get me to walk about, and some time was spent with me walking the hospital corridors with a stoma bag dangling by my side and pushing a stand upon which was my drip with large doses of antibiotics. In time the dreaded day came when the surgeon decided the stoma bag should be removed, and after a long and painful battle, it came out and the hole in my side was stitched up. Once this was done, I was discharged to a local hotel and began my chemotherapy. After a couple of sessions, it was decided that I was well enough to return to Jakarta, but Dr Tan was of the view that I should come back to Singapore weekly for further follow up sessions of chemo for a year. I really didn't fancy travelling up and down to Singapore each week missing work priorities so after some heated debate, he agreed that I could have the chemo treatment in Jakarta provided I took the medication from Singapore and that a particular Doctor in Jakarta should be put in charge of the chemo program.

I duly returned to Jakarta and met up with the recommended oncologist, and we agreed that I would visit the Jakarta Cancer Hospital every Friday morning at 6 a.m. for treatment. I decided that Friday mornings would be the best as that meant that I would have the entire weekend to recover before going back to work on the Monday. It was useful having an early start at six as before long the chemo room at the hospital was filled with really sick people, each having their chemo treatment. Cancer patients tend to bond with each other, and I became good friends with many of them. The only sad part was that by the end of my year of treatment many of them had died from the disease. The oncologist was extremely helpful, and his nursing staff were dedicated to their task. However, here was I, a foreigner and a senior diplomat to boot, and many of the nurses found administering to me quite daunting. The extent of their trauma in dealing with this white "VIP" patient was soon apparent as some of them were visibly shaking with nerves as they tried to place the needle in my vein for the drip. I think the worst occasion was when three nurses tried eight times to get the needle into my vein and left me bleeding and sore. I discussed this with the oncologist who was concerned that these unsuccessful attempts could lead to permanent damage to my veins, and it was agreed that two nurses who had proved most capable would agree between them a program whereby at least one of them would be available every Friday morning at 6. One of them was a sweet girl who wore the Islamic Jilbab (Headscarf) and prayed before inserting the needle, and the other was a male former theatre nurse who identified the vein and rammed it in. One was gentle, and the other was rough, but they both achieved success in their own style, and I owe them both a debt of gratitude.

My oncologist in Singapore was of the opinion that mental attitude was an important part of the fight against cancer, and I am convinced that my decision to return to as normal a life as possible in Jakarta, with work to keep me engaged, was just as important as the chemo treatment for my recovery. I bought a cheap set of golf clubs, as did Debra, and we went golfing every weekend on the golf course just behind our Jakarta home. Golfing did help, but my self-esteem was hit when Debra was soon able to outdrive me on the course. On a brighter note, my short game was better than hers, so we usually managed a similar score. I firmly believe that golf and a positive outlook on life played a big part in my recovery, and by the end of my year of chemotherapy, I was playing 36 holes a day on a weekend.

I still had to go back to Singapore for check-ups so that my oncologist could keep an eye on me so that I could have a colonoscopy to check that no further polyps were growing and that the joined ends of my colon were still intact. In discussions with my oncologist, I learned that genetics play an important part in the development of colon cancer and the fact that my father and his father both died from colon cancer was very relevant. My oncologist was of the opinion that colon cancer could be more easily defeated than some other cancers in that people who had a blood relative die from colon cancer could have regular colonoscopies to ensure that polyps are removed before they become cancerous. I, therefore, urge any reader who has a parent who died from colon cancer to have a colonoscopy every few years. It's essentially a painless procedure, but I have to admit that the pre-colonoscopy preparation with high doses of laxatives is a nuisance! I should add that due to genetics, my daughter Aurora is obliged to undergo colonoscopies every three years for life.

I was fortunate in that Dr Teh Lip Bin who attended to my colonoscopies was well skilled, and we soon became good friends as I was regularly on his treatment table. He conducts colonoscopies under heavy sedation and so for most people they are totally unaware of what is going on during the procedure. However, in my case, for some reason, I regularly came awake during the procedure and could watch on his TV monitor as the scope made its way through my colon. It was fascinating to watch as he lassoed any polyp that he found with a fine loop of wire then passed a current through the wire as he burnt it off from the colon wall. I always tried to identify the point at which the sedative drug took hold and I became unconscious, but I have to report that it is not possible, and one moment you are alert and chatting, and the next, you are off! I had regular, yearly, then two yearly and now three yearly colonoscopies, and am still attended to by Dr Teh after 27 years! So much for the original diagnosis that I would be lucky to survive for five years.

During my time in the Embassy in Jakarta, I was asked by the Ambassador to represent the British Government on the board of the Jakarta International School (JIS), which was the school my daughter was attending. JIS began as the Joint Embassy School and was set up by the governments of the US, the UK, Australia, and Yugoslavia for the children of their diplomats. Yugoslavia was involved as the school was set up at the height of the influence of the Non-Aligned Movement, and President Tito and President Sukarno were close friends. By the nineties, Yugoslavian representation on the board of governors had dropped and the remaining three government representatives were holding the position of "super governors" representing the interests of the founding fathers of the school. I imagined that my time on the Board of Governors would be short-lived, but little did I know that I was not going to be able to escape from the position for 15 long years.

This was a time of change and growth in Jakarta as ribbon development took place in line with the boom in the Indonesian economy. Banks were happy to lend vast sums of money to Indonesian developers until the crash of 1997, when the development stalled as the Asian Financial crisis took hold. By the middle of 1997, Indonesia's total debt to foreign banks amounted to almost 60 billion US dollars. Much of the debt was owed by projects that were controlled by the family of President Soeharto. In addition to the debt problem, the rapid development was not matched by infrastructure improvements, and Jakarta traffic began a slow slide into gridlock.

The years in Jakarta passed, and following my cancer problem I decided it was time to retire from diplomatic life and decisions had to be made as to what we would do upon my retirement. Aurora played a major role in our decision. She said that she had spent her life travelling around the world as I went from posting to posting, and she went from school to school. It was her view that JIS was the best school she had ever attended, and maintained that she wanted to spend the remaining four years of her school life at JIS. At that time, she was on the school's honor roll, and we struck a deal that provided she stayed on the honor roll, she could remain in JIS. I should perhaps add that there is another angle to this story. When Aurora was about 12 or 13 years old, Debra, who suffers from dyslexia, began to realize that Aurora was also dyslexic. In discussions with the school, it was agreed that they would carry out some tests which confirmed that she was acutely dyslexic and had the reading age of a 7-year-old. To their credit, JIS did not stop there and put her under the care of their expert counsellors and therapists, and with their help she came to grips with her condition. It is of interest that she was a classic left-handed dyslexic, as was Einstein, and whilst spelling and writing were problematic, her grades improved and she went on to pass her International Baccalaureate (IB) with flying colors.

The Private Sector

In 1997, I left government service and ventured into the private sector. Using skills from my former police service I worked as an independent consultant for mainly international companies advising them on their operations in Indonesia. This work took me back to Papua, where an international oil and gas company was conducting exploration drilling in the hinterland close to the border with Papua New Guinea. The company had two test drills about 50 kilometers apart and some 50 kilometers from their base camp, which was at the head of a river. All supplies were shipped up the river by barges and then stored to be moved on to the drill sites as required by heavy lift helicopters. Drill casings, compressors and other equipment had to be hauled slung from these helicopters as they flew over dense jungle. The remoteness of the operation presented security problems, and the company encountered problems with the local tribesmen over the compensation to be paid for trees cut down to erect the drill staging. One of my primary tasks was to ensure that the company employees understood that these Stone Age tribesmen, with their bows and arrows and stone axes, were a force to be reckoned with and had to be handled with sensitivity.

In Papua, things are never as they seem, and operating systems suited to operations in the west are totally inappropriate in the Papuan environment. During hours of darkness, the helicopters were parked on a landing pad in the centre of the base camp compound, and when I got there, I found that the security lights for these aircraft were situated on the circumference of the compound facing the helicopters. It took some time to persuade them that the lights illuminated the aircraft as a target and, in the process, stole the night vision from those inside the compound. The answer was to reposition the lights in the centre of the compound, thereby illuminating the jungle beyond the compound. The next challenge was to persuade the company that their plan to erect a high perimeter fence around the three compounds was not a good idea. The area was remote, and the OPM (Separatist Terror Group) was known to travel through that area when moving to and from Papua New Guinea. Police and military were miles away and the only real security was that provided by the villagers whose homes surrounded the compounds.

The company had two Indonesian doctors who sat in an air-conditioned portacabin all day, every day, watching satellite TV and waiting for an accident to happen. I managed after some considerable persuasion to get the company on the side of my idea to get the doctors out of the portacabins to run clinics in these villages. The doctors had to be paid for whatever they did, and the cost of drugs they prescribed was much less than the cost of the perimeter fences. The village heads were happy and the security of the operation was greatly enhanced.

Another problem was that the company used a local agent to provide the manpower the company required to cut down trees and general laboring duties. By sitting down chatting to the village headmen, I soon learned that the agent was only feeding the laborers a meagre diet of tinned sardines and rice. Knowing that the agent was well compensated for the provision of food, I arranged for the laborers to be better fed, and immediately morale improved, work output went up, and by extension, security was again enhanced.

There is no formula for dealing with unsophisticated tribesmen, but one must be prepared to use one's imagination. A case in point involved the drill sites and the real danger to villagers when the helicopters came in to land with heavy equipment swinging precariously underneath them on a cable. The drill site boss had tried to persuade the villagers not to encroach onto the work site, but they didn't seem to understand. He pointed out to me a point on the ground beyond which he didn't want them to cross, but he failed to realize that they had no understanding of an imaginary point on the ground; but when I had a simple fence constructed with saplings, they knew and understood the point of demarcation. As a further measure, I arranged that the company put a satellite-fed TV in a locked box in a tree some 200 meters into the jungle with power cables and TV feed run from the camp. The village headman was presented with the key and instructed on the operation of the TV. The villagers were never again a danger on the work site as they found watching TV infinitely more interesting than watching helicopters deliver heavy equipment.

After a year working as an independent security consultant, I set up a security consultancy company with another expat and an Indonesian businessman. The date of the company's inauguration was 1 April 1998, which is important as a mere six weeks later, Jakarta would be plunged into complete chaos by the May 1998 race riots. Our company had signed up a few multinational companies and provided them with advice and timely information on the changing security situation. The reign of President Soeharto was weakening and there were daily demonstrations on campus by university students. Eventually, the military commander General Wiranto allowed the students to demonstrate outside of the campus, and their voices became ever louder. Jakarta was like a tinder keg, and it became increasingly apparent that disorder would break out, and the only question was when.

The situation came to a head on Tuesday, 12 May, when some 6,000 students from the University of Trisakti in Central Jakarta held a nonviolent protest demanding the resignation of President Soeharto. The demonstrators lowered the Indonesian flag on the campus to half-mast, and a march to the Parliament building began at noon. The students were stopped by the police a few hundred meters from the campus, and they began a sit-in on the road. The police were then reinforced by armed military units, and a University Dean persuaded the students to return to the campus. By late afternoon most of the students had returned to the campus, but those who had not taken refuge in the campus buildings came under fire from the security forces, four of them died from gunshot wounds, and dozens more were injured.

The four students were buried the following day, and Jakarta remained on a knife edge as the gravity of the situation began to set in. During that day and the morning of Thursday 14 May, I went around the town trying to assess the situation, and by 9 a.m. on the Thursday morning, it became clear that the situation was about to take a turn for the worse. I had written a contingency plan for a five-star hotel in Jakarta and called the General Manager, advising that he get the plan out and that I would join him at the hotel within the hour.

When I wrote the plan for the hotel, it called for operations to continue with up to 120% occupancy, only one shift of staff available and no deliveries of fuel, water, and food for at least 7 days. In the event, that turned out to be the case. By the time I arrived at the hotel, racial violence had broken out with ethnic Chinese Indonesians being the main target. The General Manager and I stood on the heliport on the top of the hotel and we counted over 90 buildings on fire before the dense clouds of smoke made it impossible to count any more individual fires. The sheer scale of the riots was unbelievable and led to the death of more than 1,200 people and the rape and killing of many ethnic Chinese females.

The rest of the day was spent dealing with calls from clients who sought advice on the situation. I decided to use the hotel as my base and directed those clients who needed to seek refuge to come to that hotel where I could brief them on the rapidly changing situation. By late evening I was requested to rescue a female member of staff from a client company and my driver and I set off to collect the girl from the company office and deliver her safely to her home in South Jakarta. As we drove through the barricades of burning tires on the road, I had in my hand a bundle of low-denomination notes and instructed the driver that if we were attacked, he should not stop but attempt to get away as I threw the notes out of the rear window of the car. In the event, we were not physically attacked, and the young lady was delivered home to her anxious parents.

Whilst all this was happening, Debra was at home waiting for Aurora to come home from school. After three unsuccessful attempts, Aurora arrived home around 11 p.m. in the car of a school teacher and told how she had seen a man on a bicycle with a fridge which he had no doubt just looted. The following morning Debra and Aurora moved into the hotel with me, where they would be safe whilst I went about the business of looking after clients.

The idea of gathering all my clients at the hotel paid off and made it easy to brief them on the changing situation. By midday, on the Friday, the US State Department issued a warning notice advising US nationals to leave the country, and the governments of most Western countries followed suit. The problem was that it was unclear at that time whether the road between the centre of town and the airport was safe and secure. I arranged with the US, British and Australian Embassies that we would take turns checking out the airport road, and when it was declared to be safe, we would arrange convoys with police protection to ensure that our clients got to the airport without incident. Things were quite chaotic at the airport as many were in panic mode and desperate to leave. Some rich ethnic Chinese pulled up at the door to the airport and sold their cars off cheaply before going in to catch a flight. It was a shame that I was too busy looking after clients to take advantage of the situation! Yet, again, service before self.

The Singapore Government, conscious of the fact that ethnic Chinese were at risk organized evacuation flights for its nationals, and we decided that it would be best if Debra and Aurora took advantage of these evacuation flights. Singapore nationals simply needed to turn up at the airport with their passport and identity card and would be able to board one of several flights with no ticketing required. The Singapore government sent staff from their Ministry of Foreign Affairs to the airport to assist its nationals, and there was a surprise for Debra, as the man from the Ministry who dealt with her was her cousin! With Debra and Aurora safe in Singapore, I was able to concentrate on looking after my clients and some companies and individuals who were not my clients. Whether they were clients or not, we assisted them in leaving the country, kept in touch with them whilst they were out of the country, and later assisted them in returning to Indonesia when the situation stabilized. The decision not to turn away people who were not clients was the right one, certainly from a moral point of view, but also from a business point of view, as they all signed contracts with us after they returned.

The days immediately after the riots were tense, and the military patrolled the streets with armored vehicles and tanks, desperately trying to bring law and order back. The military allowed the students to occupy Parliament, and on Saturday, 20 May, the Chief of the military, General Wiranto, told President Soeharto that he no longer had the support of the military. The following day Soeharto resigned, and the Deputy President Dr Habibie took over. This took the heat out of the situation and within a week, things were beginning to get back to normal. It was to be some time, however, before the effects of the riots disappeared, and many years later, windows in some buildings remained broken from the rioting. A government spokesman later reported that the riots led to the destruction of over 1,600 shops, close to 400 offices, 65 banks, 12 hotels, 40 shopping malls, 2,500 shop houses and over 1,000 homes. His report also pointed out that in addition to the ethnic Chinese who were murdered, many poor citizens died when buildings they were looting caught fire, and they perished in the fire.

One postscript of the rioting was the relationship we managed to develop with the Indonesian National Police. We were able to sign Memorandum of Understanding (MOU) agreements with the police so that officers about to retire could be released to work with us in order that we might ease their way into the private sector. It was also agreed that young NCOs from the Police Mobile Brigade (swat and tactical police unit) would be attached to us to give them wider exposure as part of their career development. These MOUs were advantageous both to my company and the police, and as Indonesia lurched forward along the path of democracy following the fall of Soeharto this police presence was to become a real plus.

The country more or less meandered along under the Presidency of Dr Habibie, but behind the scenes, political moves were being engineered in advance of the forthcoming legislative elections. The transition to a more democratic form of government was not entirely smooth, and by the middle of 1999, friction between students and the security authorities resurfaced. In September, things took a turn for the worse and serious student demonstrations broke out in Jakarta, Bali and Surabaya. There were many reasons for the student unrest, but a major fly in the ointment was a new security law which gave the military greater powers which the students saw as a return to the undemocratic methods employed under Soeharto. In Jakarta, over 10,000 students took to the streets and clashed with the police and military along the major roads in the centre of the capital. The security authorities used water cannons, rubber bullets and tear gas to disperse the students, but at least one of the three students killed died from gunshot wounds.

By this time, we had moved into a penthouse apartment in the middle of town, which gave us a great view of the incidents during the unrest. Such was the commanding view from our 33rd floor apartment that Aurora was able to relay to me developments on the streets as the student demonstrators attacked the Parliament building, and we were able to put this information out to our clients. Indeed, on one occasion, Aurora came out of the shower with a towel wrapped around her, only to be confronted by almost the entire Defense Department of the US Embassy, who were using our apartment as an observation post!

The young NCOs who were working with us were excellent providers of intelligence as they scoured the streets in plain clothes and were able to report on developments as they happened. One of them hitched a ride in a jeep that was moving from the centre of town out to the Parliament building following the students, and when the vehicle was obliged to stop a few hundred yards from the Parliament complex, he got out of the vehicle and walked ahead to take a photo of the jeep – a move that was to save his life. As he did so, a bomb that had been hidden in the vehicle exploded, killing all on board and whilst he was injured in the blast, the bomb was in the rear of the vehicle and the jeep engine shielded him from much of the shrapnel. However, his lower legs were severely damaged, and he was hospitalized for some time. Others who remained in the vehicle died from their injuries. Debra, Aurora and I went to visit him in hospital and such was his character that he struggled to sit up and salute as we entered his hospital room. I am delighted to say that he made a complete recovery and went on to spend many more years with us.

The Parliamentary elections came and went with little reaction, with the PDI-P party of President Sukarno's daughter, Megawati, winning the election but without a complete majority and being obliged to enter into a coalition with the Muslim PKB party. Megawati had her eyes on the Presidency, but as the October Presidential elections approached, she was one of three candidates, the other two being the head of the PKB party, Gus Dur, and Dr Habibie, who was running for re-election. However, Parliament rejected Habibie's accountability speech on his presidency, and he withdrew, leaving Megawati and Gus Dur to fight it out. In the event, Gus Dur won narrowly and Megawati's supporters began to riot. Realising the danger of these riots escalating, Gus Dur persuaded General Wiranto to withdraw from the Vice Presidential race, and Megawati stood and won the position of Vice President.

Indonesia Age of Terrorism

After these elections, things began to quieten down in Indonesia in general, and Jakarta in particular, as people became used to democratic rule and the economy began to recover. However, this reflective calm was shattered on 1 August 2000 when there was a terrorist attack on the Philippines Ambassador to Indonesia. The Ambassador's car was turning into his residence in the centre of town when it was hit by a huge blast from a bomb in a parked car on the street. The bomb killed two bystanders and injured 21 others, including the Ambassador. There was much speculation as to who was behind the bombing, and the two main terror groups in the Philippines, the Moro Islamic Liberation Front and the Abu Sayyaf Group, both denied responsibility and it would be some time before it became clear that the bombing was the work of the Indonesian terrorist group Jemaah Islamiyah (JI). This was a totally unexpected incident and marked the beginning of more than a decade of terrorist bombings in Indonesia.

On Christmas Eve 2000, Debra, Aurora and I, together with many diplomatic personnel, went to the midnight service at the Vatican Embassy, and as we came out of the service and were chatting to the many diplomats that we knew, I switched my pager back on and got a message from my company Control Room to the effect that there had been some bombings of churches in several cities around midnight. I immediately informed the Nuncio and other diplomats. The Nuncio was shocked and decided that he had better report immediately to the Vatican, and we beat a hasty retreat to the safety of our home. By next morning, the situation became clearer, and we learned that there had been 38 bombing incidents in churches in 11 cities throughout the archipelago killing 19 and wounding 120. The choice of churches as targets for these bombings tended to suggest that a Muslim group was involved, but it was not clear who the perpetrators were. (There had always been violence against Christians in Indonesia, and between 1969 and 2007 some 950 churches were vandalized or burnt down but never bombed.)

Needless to say, the bombings led to an increased interest in our services by multinational companies, mainly in the oil and gas and mining sectors where they had operations in far-flung places, and we were kept quite busy, but little did we know just how busy we would later become due to terror attacks by Islamic groups. Life in Indonesia went on as democracy took its faltering steps and the economy began to recover. Building sites that came to a halt in 1997 were resurrected and President Gus Dur, a half blind former senior cleric, preached that anti-ethnic Chinese feelings should be brought to an end, and ethnic Indonesian Chinese were allowed to read and write Chinese script again, a thing that had been banned by Soeharto who saw them as a fifth column.

There was a normality and sense of wellbeing that was about to be shattered in July 2001 when President Gus Dur was impeached and removed from power with some 40,000 Indonesian troops surrounding the Presidential Palace, and Vice President Megawati was installed as the fifth President of the Republic. It must be stated that Gus Dur was an excellent cleric but poorly equipped to be the President of Indonesia. I must say that I admired Gus Dur when he was a cleric and later still when as the former head of an Islamic political group, he ended the policy of holding ethnic Chinese Indonesians as second-class citizens. This almost blind man had a great sense of humor, and this was illustrated when he was asked what he thought of the sexy dancing known as drilling by Inul Daratista, which many Muslims considered pornographic and therefore haram (forbidden) in Islam. He said with a grin that he saw nothing wrong with it!

There was then a period of relative calm until 12 October 2002 when a series of bombings were carried out on the tourist island of Bali, killing more than 200 and injuring hundreds of others. Around 11 p.m., a suicide bomber detonated a bomb inside Paddy's Bar in the main tourist area of Kuta. This bomb killed a few, but more seriously, it drove those who were able to run to pour out into the street where they were struck by a huge bomb that was hidden in a parked minivan outside the Sari Club on the other side of the road. At the same time, a small bomb exploded outside the

US Consulate in the Bali capital Denpasar causing minor injuries only to one person.

A huge effort was set in place to deal with the casualties, and several members of the Australian Federal Police who were in Bali either on official business or attending a Rugby 10-a-side tournament volunteered their services to assist with the injured. The Commissioner of the Australian Federal Police, Mike Keelty, contacted President Megawati and formally offered the assistance of the Federal Police which Megawati immediately accepted. It should be noted that the vast majority of those killed and injured were Australian Nationals, and a huge operation was then mounted by the Australian authorities, who flew men and forensic materials into Bali and flew many of the injured back to Australia for treatment. The Indonesian National Police, assisted by friendly countries, mounted an investigation into the bombings, and eventually, several members of JI were indicted and three were sentenced to death by firing squad.

The investigations into the Bali Bombings revealed that the attack on the Philippines Ambassador and the Christmas Eve attacks on the churches were also the work of JI, and the Indonesian authorities set up a dedicated counter-terrorist unit in the Police known as Densus 88. It was a wake-up call for companies operating in Indonesia, which meant a lot more business for security companies like mine. We began a program of carrying out risk assessments for clients and, arising from that, preparing contingency plans to deal with emergencies.

With the hotel I used during the 1998 riots, I spent considerable time trying to convince them that investment in security made sense. I made the point that there was not much difference between five-star hotels. Their rooms are similar, their food outlets much the same, and their properties are usually of a high standard. Therefore, following the Bali bombing, enhanced security provisions and improved contingency plans would make them stand out from the rest. I promised that for every dollar they invested in security, they would reap at least five dollars in increased business. In the end, I convinced them, and they did invest in greater security, and this paid off as their occupancy rate for the next 10 years was always well over 90%.

It was always my conviction that in Indonesia there were three factors that had to be considered when addressing the security of a company's operations. The first consideration was the relationship the company had with its staff. If their staff were discontented, then they would have security problems, be they strikes, reputational damage or sabotage of operations. Secondly, what was the company's relationship with the community in which its operations were situated? The relationship with the local community is crucial to the security of the operations of the company. During the 1998 riots, a western company faced a problem when a mob approached their factory, intent on burning it to the ground. The local people surrounded the plant and told the mob that the factory owners were good employers and that the company operation was in effect their economic lifeline. In the end, they convinced the mob who left them untouched and moved on elsewhere to carry out their nefarious acts. The third and final factor is what is the company's relationship with the authorities, be they police, military or local politicians? This relationship needs continuous and careful attention, but this investment of time and effort will pay off. It can be difficult to persuade a western company that its generic contingency plans, which are ideally suited to operational security in the west, will rarely be suitable for developing countries. And so it was that on our advice, the hotel in question ensured that its non-skilled employees were recruited from the area immediately behind the hotel, thus providing hotel security extra eyes and ears provided by their neighbors. A simple yet highly effective means of ensuring a holistic solution to security requirements.

Following the 1998 riots and in the spirit of mutual assistance that prompted the joint patrols of the airport road, I decided that my company would supply our security information package free to the UK, US and Australian Embassies. This does not suggest that their intelligence was so poor that they could not make sensible policies without our information. Rather, my aim in providing the information was to ensure that they were aware of the sort of information that we were providing to our commercial clients, which in a way, was a mirror of what these commercial companies saw as their information needs.

When I initially retired from Government service, I decided that I still wanted to do my bit for the expatriate community in general and the British Community in particular. When I was in the Embassy, I was an ex officio member of the British Chamber of Commerce, and regularly sat in on their board meetings as an Embassy expert on security matters. Once I retired from government service, I joined the Chamber as an ordinary member, and in addition to attending Chamber events, I became the Chair of a group of small and medium enterprise businesses that met weekly under the auspices of the Chamber. This was a role that I was to undertake for 14 years and led to my becoming more and more involved in Chamber activities to the degree that I stood for election to the Board of Governors of the Chamber and served as a Governor for eight years until I eventually retired and left Indonesia.

Whilst my company represented many British Companies, the majority of our clients were Fortune 500 companies from the United States. I, therefore, regularly attended the American Chamber of Commerce functions as a guest and got to know the Board members well. This also fitted in well with the fact that after leaving the Embassy, I continued to serve on the Board of Governors of the Jakarta International School, the majority of whose pupils were from the USA. When I sought to join the American Chamber there was a bit of difficulty as I was not an American citizen and, being self-employed, did not work for an American company. However, my perseverance paid off, and I was eventually able to become a nonvoting member of the American Chamber. Through my involvement with the American Chamber, I came into contact with the Indonesian chapter of the Overseas Security Advisory Council (OSAC). OSAC was created by Ronald Reagan's Secretary of State, George Schultz, to promote an open dialogue between the US Government and the American private sector on security issues overseas. OSAC has a network of Country Councils around the world that act as an interface between the US Administration and American business overseas. There was a Country Council in Indonesia, and I regularly attended their meetings and occasionally was invited to give presentations on security issues. In time, I was invited by the US Embassy Regional Security Officer (RSO) to become a member of the board of the Country Council, and became more and more deeply involved in their activities. After some years and several JI bombings, I was invited to take up the appointment of Vice Chair of the Country Council and served in that capacity for some eight years. (I was unable to be appointed Chair as, again, I was not a US citizen and did not work for a US company.) One of my more onerous duties was to write the monthly security report that ran to around 40 pages and was circulated to the OSAC membership and OSAC HQ. However, I must say that the United States Embassy, and by extension, the U.S. Department of Foreign Affairs, appreciated my efforts and were happy to say so in public as well as private. Indeed, they presented me with plaques and testimonials when I eventually left Indonesia.

There was great concern amongst the membership of OSAC concerning the security of the Jakarta International School, as most of the students were from Western countries. I was tasked with reviewing the security of the school, both as an OSAC board member and as a governor of the school. After a series of meetings with the Indonesian security authorities, I decided in conjunction with the Board of Governors and the school authorities to call a town hall meeting at the school at which I outlined the threat posed to the school as a target of the JI terror group and the proposed changes in security at the school. Many of the parents objected to the proposed restrictions on access to the school grounds, largely based on what they conceived as inconvenience. I argued that convenience was the enemy of security, and after a stormy session and with support from the US Embassy, it was agreed that the new restrictive measures would be applied and would be supervised by a member of my company staff to ensure compliance. In the fullness of time, our new restrictions proved to be a sensible move as a JI operator under interrogation admitted that the school had been a target of the JI, but was dropped when the new restrictions made it too difficult a target. I am indebted to those parents who accepted the need to tighten access to the campus.

One thing I did learn from the American Chamber and OSAC was the value of "Town Hall Meetings" as a means of briefing groups on vital security issues. I adopted this system with my own company, and town hall meetings for our valued clients became a regular means of ensuring that they were well briefed on security issues likely to affect their operations.

One such town hall meeting took place on 20 March 2003 when I gathered my clients together in a five-star hotel for a briefing on the Bush/Blair invasion of Iraq. This briefing was arranged at the last minute and came about as a result of numerous requests from clients who felt the need to be briefed as they feared there could be some blowback to their operations in Indonesia. The briefing began as the tanks were rolling into Iraq, and we were lucky to have as a guest speaker a former weapons inspector in Iraq who was about to join my company as a consultant. It was great to have someone with that degree of knowledge able to speak in a most knowledgeable way, not only on Iraq in general but also on the weapons of mass destruction issue. He was able to say with confidence that in his view, no weapons of mass destruction would be found, and no Scud missiles would be fired. He knew for a fact that their gyroscopes were not operational, and the Scud force was essentially grounded.

The hotel had provided a projector system, and we were able to watch TV coverage of the invasion on a large screen which meant that the meeting went on and on, and after lunch, we resumed. Such was the interest that by the end of the day, there were still a few hardy souls who were keen to continue, and we moved on to the hotel bar, where a lively discussion took place on the rights and wrongs of the invasion. I suspect that little did we realize at the time just what a dreadful mistake the invasion was and how it would lead to the situation with ISIS, where Sunni Muslims felt betrayed by the Shiite minority government, as did the Kurds. The country was effectively split into three, as was predicted by Richard Clarke, the U.S. National Coordinator for Security and Counter terrorism, whose advice was ignored by President George Bush and who resigned soon after the invasion. Much has been written on how Tony Blair was dragged along on the coattails of George Bush into a fool's war, and I do not intend to regurgitate it here but suffice it to say that with all his faults, Saddam Hussein effectively managed to keep the Iranians in their box and his firm (some might say harsh) rule kept inter-faith problems from arising. What is clear, however, is that for Tony Blair the special relationship between the US and the UK became, in the words of Sir Christopher Meyer, "an end in itself" and led Blair to promise Bush that whatever he decided, he would have the full support of the UK.

In the event, there were no severe repercussions in the world's largest Muslim nation on the invasion of Iraq and life in Indonesia in general, and Jakarta in particular, went on. Many of the security checks put in place after the Bali bombing began to wither on the vine as apathy set in and the memories of the Bali Bombing faded. One of the major problems facing a company such as mine is how to persuade clients in a period of relative calm to continue taking sensible precautions and not to let their guard down. This apathy was about to be shattered by the bombing of the J W Marriott Hotel in Jakarta on 5 August 2003, just two days before the court verdict was due in the Bali Bombing case. A suicide bomber drove a Toyota Kijang motor vehicle up the hotel's driveway, almost to the front door, where he detonated a bomb in the vehicle, killing 12 and injuring 150. The blast was such that a crater was blown in the concrete of the driveway, and the bomber's severed head was found on the fifth floor of the hotel. The timing suggested that this was once again the work of JI which was later confirmed and sent shock waves through the expatriate community of Jakarta.

One of the major problems when tasked with securing a property in the middle of a city is what I call local geography. By this I mean the property's physical situation, the amount of standoff it enjoys from public areas and the overall vulnerability of the property. This vulnerability is increased when dealing with buildings that are by their very nature open to the public, such as hotels. Hotels need to walk the fine line between providing an adequate level of security for their guests whilst at the same time avoiding making security checks so onerous that they avoid staying there.

However, the bombing allowed me to reinforce my advice to my hotel clients that security checks at hotels were essential and good governance. I experienced some difficulty after the Bali bombing in that some hotel clients viewed Bali as being a long way off, and the situation did not justify the expense and inconvenience of security checks. I argued that terrorists thrive on publicity, and Bali was chosen for attack because it had publicity value. It was clear that Jakarta had a similar publicity value and could well be the location of other bombings. Furthermore, the ultimate aim of JI was to establish an Islamic Caliphate in South East Asia, and as part of that process, they wanted to destabilize the Indonesian economy in an attempt to bring down the government. Whilst the majority of large hotels in Jakarta were essentially in Indonesian ownership, the fact that many were under management by a Western company was enough to make them an attractive target. It was, therefore, my advice that terrorists could well strike again in Bali and also again in Jakarta.

There is a real need for hotel security staff to be well-trained and aware of the sensitivity of their actions. I always used to teach security staff of client hotels that they are not just there to check baggage or check for weapons in the manner of an automaton, but they are essentially the final arbiter of whether a guest is a bona fide person or a potential terrorist or thief. They need to study the body language of the person, looking for signs of nervousness; are they dressed appropriately, or do they appear out of place in the surroundings of a five-star hotel? I found this training of security guards to be most cost effective, not only in terms of improving their skills, but it also boosted their self-esteem and morale. At the same time, I pressed my hotel clients to update and improve their baggage scanning machines and to ensure that their security officers were properly trained in the operations of these machines. A further improvement was brought about by introducing a system of penetration tests carried out by my staff working undercover, posing as hotel guests or vendors. Advance notice of the penetration testing was limited to a few senior members of the hotel management who were sworn to secrecy to maintain the validity of the test. The scenarios used for these tests varied: Some were based on actual penetrations by role playing terrorists, and others were constructed to bring out teaching points during the wash-up of the tests. The wash-ups were extremely important, and we ensured that all security staff and senior hotel management took part in the wash-ups so that the lessons learned were circulated as widely as possible. I was at pains to stress to the hotel management that security staff should not be censured for failing a test as failure often resulted from a lack of training. That said, staff that did spot the penetration were to be rewarded in some way. In effect, there was no right or wrong by the staff, but the tests were designed to identify any flaws in the hotel security procedures or to point out the latest methods used by terrorists and common thieves to beat the hotel security system.

Following the Marriott attack, it was clear to professionals in the security and risk business that further attacks were likely, and it was not a question of if but when. In the year following that attack, I was at pains to ensure that my clients kept the danger of other attacks in mind and did not fall into the trap of complacency.

This advice proved to be prophetic as on 9 September 2004, a one-ton bomb exploded outside the Australian Embassy in the Kuningan District of Jakarta, killing nine people and injuring more than 150 others. The blast was such that other buildings in the vicinity of the Embassy were badly damaged within a radius of 500 meters. The bomb was packed inside a delivery van driven by a suicide bomber. Once again, the terrorist organization Jemaah Islamiyah (JI) claimed responsibility for the attack. The authorities claimed that two Malaysian terrorists Dr Azahari Husin and Noordin Mohammad bin Top were suspected of being involved in the planning of the attack and the assembly of the bomb. A series of arrests followed, and the police stated that one of those arrested claimed that the funds for the bombing were supplied via a courier by Osama bin Laden.

Once again increased attacks in Jakarta swept away complacency and the increase in security in the capital led the terrorists to turn their attention once again to Bali and on 1 October 2005 three bombs exploded in Bali, claiming the lives of 20 people and injuring more than 100. The first two bombs exploded near an outdoor food court on the beach at Jimbaran Bay, and the third went off ten minutes later in a restaurant in Kuta Town Square. Both target locations were frequented by tourists and were a reflection of the desire of JI to damage the Indonesian economy as part of their aim to set up a caliphate in South East Asia centered on Indonesia. The police immediately shut down the mobile telephone network in Bali (initiation of bombs by mobile phones were often used by terrorists as a backup to suicide bombers). In the event, all three blasts were carried out by suicide bombers and three unexploded devices were later discovered in the Jimbaran Bay area. Once again, the police reported that they suspected that Husin and Top were behind the attacks.

With bombing attacks having taken place in Jakarta and Bali one year apart over a four-year period, there was once again heightened security in both locations, and it was not difficult to persuade clients to review their security arrangements and be on alert. However, after four years passed following the Jimbaran and Kuta explosions without an attack taking place, complacency once again set in and on 17 July 2009, two bombing attacks by suicide bombers were carried out in Jakarta when the J W Marriott Hotel and the Ritz Carlton hotels were bombed in the space of five minutes killing nine and injuring over 50.

The bomb in the Marriott went off first in a private room serving breakfast to members of a branch of the American Chamber of Commerce. The bomb in the Ritz Carlton went off in a second-floor restaurant whilst breakfast was being served, causing extensive damage to the hotel facade. Police investigations revealed that the bombs were smuggled into the hotels the day before the attack, assisted by a terror sympathizer who worked for an outlet that served both hotels. Furthermore, a second bomb was discovered in a room in the Marriott hotel, which was programmed to go off prior to the other Marriott bomb, but it malfunctioned. It is believed that the plan was for this bomb in a hotel room to cause panic and cause guests to flee to the lobby area in the vicinity of the second bomb. Once again, the police believed that the bombing was the work of JI bomber Noordin Mohammad bin Top.

Yet again, the business community in Jakarta was put on alert and advised to review their security and business continuity plans. There were no bombings in Jakarta for a further two years, but in April 2011, a suicide bomber detonated a device in a mosque in West Java during Friday prayers injuring 30 people and six months later, another suicide bomber detonated a bomb in a church in Solo in Central Java.

Thereafter, there was a lull in terrorist activity, and it was a pleasure to return to a more settled way of life. The experience in defending against terrorist attacks grew out of having served in Northern Ireland, Sri Lanka, and Indonesia, and it provided me with sufficient knowledge to ensure that I could provide my clients with suitable advice and guidance. It became clear that the doctrine of the 7 Ps was essential, whereby prior planning and preparation prevents pretty poor performance! An understanding of the threat, followed by suitable planning, was key and was a solid platform to work from. Thereafter, it was very much a question of common sense coupled with an ability to think outside the box. When the terror activities and social unrest started, most of my client companies were unprepared, and it took a lot of education and explanation to bring them up to speed. The secret lies in a structured approach.

In addition to serving the security interests of my clients, we continued to enjoy our family life in Jakarta. In spite of the problems caused by traffic jams, life in Jakarta had its good points. We had a wide circle of friends and a very healthy social life. Freed from the diplomatic demands, we were able to live a normal existence outside of office hours, and we made the most of it.

On 19 March 2006, the President of Singapore, S R Nathan, paid a State Visit to Indonesia, and his first engagement on that visit was to attend a Reception with members of the Singapore Community in Jakarta. Debra was a prominent member of the Singapore Women's Group (SWG) in Jakarta and, being a former Miss Singapore, was asked by the wife of the Ambassador to officially welcome him to the reception. This she duly did, and our daughter and I accompanied her. When the President turned to greet me, I said how nice it was to meet up again after 30 years. He said that he was flattered that I should remember him! Such is the down-to-earth and humble approach that he brought to the position of President of the Republic of Singapore. Later in the evening, Mrs. Nathan asked Debra and Aurora to join her at her table.

President S R Nathan with Debra, Aurora and I at the Reception

We were members of a club less than a mile from our apartment, which gave us access to a first-class gym and good restaurants and a well-stocked bar. We were also members of the Shangri-La club and as such, enjoyed preferential rates when dining in the hotel and again access to a first-class gym and swimming pool on the hotel grounds. In fact, I went to the gym every morning, including Sundays and worked out for an hour before having breakfast and then going straight to the office. We made full use of the other hotel facilities and enjoyed a champagne brunch in the fine dining restaurant every Sunday for 12 years. In fact, we had a permanent booking for the same table and only rang up if we were unable to attend. The champagne brunch was extremely popular, and we made friends with many patrons who, like us, were regular attendees. It was a leisurely event where one was able to eat and drink without haste, with the brunch lasting 4 or 5 hours. The free flow of wine was incredible, with champagne to start with, then white wine before red with the main courses. The staff got to know us well, and the hotel even provided us with silver napkin rings inscribed with our names and we enjoyed service above and beyond what could be expected. In the middle of the 12-year period, the restaurant closed for several months for renovation, and we were obliged to patronize other hotel brunches. We regularly used restaurants in three other 5-star hotels, and they all tried hard to entice us to become their regular customers, but our allegiance to the Shangri-La was too strong and return we did.

These brunches were akin to a dining club, and the regulars became good friends. One elderly couple were regulars, and we got to know them from meeting at the brunches. They were kind enough to bring several of their domestic helpers along to join them for brunch. Over a period of time, we learned that their domestic staff all came from the same village and that they had no children and that when they passed on, all their wealth would be given over to their staff. One Sunday during lunch, they invited us to join them for dinner the following Friday at their Jakarta home in a very posh area of the city. They greeted us warmly and gave us a guided tour of their very large well-appointed home, which spread over four floors with elevators between floors. They were Roman Catholics and had a chapel in the home where a local priest held a private service for them from time to time. They also had a fully fitted Japanese restaurant, and brought a local chef in to service this restaurant when required for entertaining friends. We enjoyed a fabulous meal, and over dinner, he explained that he was a civil engineer and had spent most of his career in the USA. His wife became disabled with spinal problems and was confined to a wheelchair. When this happened, he sold off a few of his Beverly Hills mansions, and they relocated to Jakarta, where he designed and built his own house.

That was typical of Indonesia, where many of the almost 300 million population were very poor, and the rich were very rich. On one occasion, we were invited to dinner by a wealthy businessman who owned a large mansion in the middle of a golf course, and he took great pleasure in giving us a guided tour before dinner. The large garden had refrigerated mist systems which allowed him to grow plants from temperate climates, and the mansion had a separate building which served as an art gallery for his extensive collection. Over dinner, we were joined by the then current Miss Universe and actor Bruce Willis. This was typical Indonesian dislocation of expectation.

Aurora's Higher Education

I continued as a governor of the Jakarta International School (JIS), which Aurora attended until 2001, when she went off to study psychology at the University of Nottingham. During her early months at the university, she realised how well-prepared she was compared to her fellow students. Not only had JIS served her well, but the International Baccalaureate (IB) she completed in her final two years at JIS, ensured that she was well prepared for reading for a degree.

I had always told her that, like I did in my youth, she should regard attending university as a full-time job and work a full 8-hour day. You can imagine how shocked I was when she said she was pub crawling with her friends almost every night in her first few weeks. I immediately scolded her, but she soon put me right by explaining that JIS had prepared her so well that she was already ahead of her peers at university.

She enjoyed her B.Sc. course so much that she asked if she could stay on and read for a Master's in Occupational Psychology. We agreed, and she passed her Master's degree with merit. Fired up by her performance on the Master's course, she decided that she wanted to remain at university and aim for a PhD in Applied Psychology. We, of course, agreed but insisted that she no longer live in shared student accommodation, and we purchased a house for her in Long Eaton in the East Midlands, thereby providing her with a secure and settled location for her advanced studies. She applied herself to her studies and worked diligently on her thesis. We were, therefore, not surprised when she was duly awarded a PhD for her efforts.

The Graduation of Dr Aurora Watters

After a period of rest, she began looking for suitable positions in the UK, but she was headhunted by the Government of Singapore, who called her out of the blue and interviewed her for four hours by a long-distance telephone call. That was followed up by a face-to-face interview in London by two representatives of the Singapore Government, who offered her a position as a Researcher in a government think tank, a position which she happily took up, and moved to Singapore.

Her Doctorate equipped her well for her position, and she applied herself diligently. She was later promoted to Senior

Researcher and before long, was running seminars and presentations attended by large groups of participants.

Retirement

Essentially having served in the British Embassy in Jakarta for four years and provided input to the security interests of our clients in Indonesia for 15 years, we decided that as I had reached the age of 70 years, it was time to move forward into retirement. We held family discussions on where we should aim to spend the rest of our life and eventually decided we would retire to Malacca. When I was posted to the British High Commission in Singapore in 1977, I spent many weekends in Malacca as the single staff members in our High Commissions in Singapore and Malaysia met up in Malacca for weekend parties. Furthermore, Debra's mother came from Malacca, and Debra felt a warmth for the town, so it was an easy decision.

Malacca is a fantastic place for retirement being situated on the Strait of Malacca with fabulous beaches and a multitude of wonderful restaurants and food stalls providing Malay, Chinese, Indian and Portuguese Eurasian foods.

Sunset over the Strait of Malacca

One great advantage of moving to Malacca was that we were able to join the Malacca Club, which is a private members club with a location in town which had a restaurant and a large function room, but it also had an out-of-town location a few minutes' drive from our home. This country facility is located on the Strait of Malacca with excellent views across the Straits and has full sporting facilities, including swimming pools and open-air dining, which are perfect for tropical living.

The Swimming Complex at the Malacca Club

We moved to Malacca in 2011 and began house hunting which was a herculean task. After we had been searching for three months, we were having coffee in the office of the Manager of the HSBC bank in Malacca, when he asked how the house hunting was going. Debra explained that we were not having much success, so he asked us to set out our requirements. This we did, and he telephoned an estate agent friend of his and gave him our requirements list. The agent said he did not have a house that suited our requirements but promised to look out for us. The very next day, the bank manager called to say that his agent had identified a suitable property, and we went off to visit it. It did, in fact, meet most of our requirements in that it was a single-story detached house, on a corner plot with a large garden, but was quite run down. However, after some negotiations, we did manage to purchase the property, which we planned to modernize and extend.

The purchase took some time, as did the planning by the architect and the building work by a contractor, but we did manage to move into the house in April 2012. It is worthy of note that the house was in fact built as officer-married quarters by the British military and was situated right opposite the satay stall that I used to frequent in 1977, on my visits to Malacca from Singapore. It was also identical to a house in another part of Malacca in which Debra's Grandmother lived. What a small world!

The house prior to renovation and extension

The house after renovation

Monkeys in our garden

A short distance from our house and on the way to the Malacca Club is an establishment known as Bert's Garden, which is a restaurant and bar. Prior to Covid, it was a regular watering hole as my local bar, where I could sit with friends enjoying a drink whilst overlooking the Straits of Malacca.

The view from the bar

A great advantage of retiring to Malacca was that Debra was able to travel to Singapore often to see her mother and other family members. In turn, they were also able to travel from Singapore to Malacca in about 4 hours and visit us.

Debra at her mother's home

Aurora Marries Luke Watts

When Aurora was studying for her PhD degree at Nottingham University, she met a young man named Luke Watts, who hailed from the Midlands. After her return to Singapore, they conducted a long-distance relationship until 25 November 2017, when he proposed to her over dinner on the Singapore Flier. They decided that they would get married in Malacca in St Peters Church, which is the same church where Debra's parents were married all those years ago. With Aurora living in Singapore and the wedding taking place in Malacca, the planning for the event was clearly going to present many logistical problems. After much discussion, it was decided that Debra would take over the role of a wedding planner and I must say that her organizational skills were outstanding, and the wedding was, without doubt, the wedding of the year in Malacca with the reception taking place in the Hilton Hotel.

The marriage was between a Singaporean and an Englishman, and with the bride's parents being Singaporean and Scottish, it became a transnational affair. The timing was also important as the date of the wedding was the day before the 40TH wedding anniversary of Debra and me. So as midnight approached, the wedding party moved on to become an anniversary party.

I must point out that prior to the actual wedding reception, there was a very well-kept secret in that Debra had arranged for a quintet of Pipers and drummers from a Kuala Lumpur based Sikh Pipe band to play the bridal party into the ballroom and then, finally with the grand entrance of the bride and groom with the entire room getting to their feet and applauding the couple. Thereafter, they played for the guests a selection of tunes, including a Portuguese Eurasian folk song (Jinkli Nona) which had all the Eurasian guests on their feet in ecstasy! I should point out that this Sikh Pipe Band actually came to play in a pipe band competition at the Jakarta Highland Gathering in the 1990s when I was on the organizing committee of the Gathering. We got to know them then and have kept in touch over all the years since.

The placing of the veil

Family outside St Peter's Church

My moment of pride and sadness

In August 2021, I was prescribed a new drug for an enlarged prostate gland my body did not react well to and I suffered from dizzy spells. I went back to see the doctor who had prescribed it, but after sitting and waiting to see him for three hours, I decided to return home, and Debra noticed that I was having trouble walking with my right leg dragging along the ground. Debra suspected that I was suffering from a stroke, and I went off to see a Neurosurgeon who suspected a stroke and after brain scans, blood tests and x-rays, he confirmed that I had suffered a slight stroke, but it was a mild stroke, and there was no bleeding in the brain. He suspected that the prostrate medicine had caused a severe drop in my blood pressure that led to the stroke and advised that I should go on a low-fat diet, begin an exercise regime and check my blood pressure three times a day. I did as he suggested and after two years, I am now working out for close to one hour every morning on an exercise bike and have lost over 20 kilos weight. My cardiovascular system is much improved, my heart rate during exercise is much reduced, and recovery time after exercise is almost immediate.

Whilst Covid put an end to Debra's monthly trips to Singapore, we managed to travel to Singapore in June 2022 to celebrate her mother's 95th birthday, and a few weeks later, her mother, together with her sister Sharon and husband Ken, came to Malacca for a few days.

Debra, her mother and sister Sharon walking along the Strait of Malacca

Round In a Full Circle

Readers may wonder why we retired to Malacca and the answer is simple. As mentioned earlier, Debra's Mother was born in Malacca and her family has strong roots in Malacca stretching over generations. Her mother was the youngest daughter of a man who played a major role in the development of Malacca in general and its Portuguese Eurasians in particular. I am referring to:

The Honorable Vincent Emanuel Dias

Chevalier of the Order of the Silver Cross

of the Imperial Order of Portugal

Malayan Certificate of Honor (MCH)

Justice of the Peace (JP)

Fellow of the Royal Society of the Arts (FRSA)

The Honorable Vincent Emanuel Dias MCH, JP
wearing the Order of the Silver Cross of the Imperial Order
of Portugal

Debra's Grandfather was a man of many talents but he was also a man who devoted himself to the people of Malaya, as it was then, and served in a variety of roles in the British administration of Malaya ending as the Office Assistant in the office of the British Resident Commissioner.

The following lists just some of the roles that he played in the community:

Justice of the Peace.

Chief Warden at St Peter's Church.

Member of the Board of Administration, St Peter's Church.

Committee Member of the Vinolia Association.

Honorary Auditor of the Straits Union Club.

Fellow of the British Royal Society of Arts.

Secretary of the Malacca Recreation Association.

Member of the Committee of the Malacca Government and Municipal Servants' Co-operative Thrift and Loan Society.

Acted as an intermediary between the British Resident Councilor and the Catholic Church in the setting up of the Portuguese Settlement in Malacca.

Committee Member of the Malacca Football Association.

Honorary Secretary of the Malacca Recreation Club.

Committee Member of the Junior Civil Service Association.

Company Quartermaster Sergeant D Company of the Malayan Volunteer Corps.

President of the Eurasian Association.

Member of the Committee of the Malacca Coronation Celebrations.

Presented with the British Coronation Medal for his public services over the years.

President of the Malacca Historical Association.

Awarded the Malayan Certificate of Honor in recognition of his loyal and valuable services to the country.

October 1943 to December 1944 was imprisoned by the Japanese Occupying Forces.

1945 returned to work as the Office Assistant in the Malacca Secretariat.

1946 – Retires from Government service after 40 years of service.

Eurasian member on the Board of Commissioners.

Assistant Secretary of the Settlement Defense Committee.

19th May 1951 was knighted by the Portuguese Government for his services to the Eurasian community in Malaya with the title Chevalier of the Order of the Silver Cross of the Imperial Order of Portugal.

1951 Elected Municipal Commissioner.

Vice President of the Malacca Labor Party.

Member of the reception committee for the visit of His Royal Highness Prince Edward, the Duke of Kent and his mother, Her Royal Highness Princess Marina, the Duchess of Kent to Malacca.

A Settlement Commissioner and Municipal Councilor and was elected Municipal Vice President and Labor Councilor for the Tranquerah Ward of the Malacca Municipality.

A man who really put service before self and so this book has come full circle.

Made in the USA
Middletown, DE
09 August 2024

58517938R00126